I0605755

SOUTH AFRICA

BY SUE BRADFORD EDWARDS

An Imprint of Abdo Publishing
abdobooks.com

ABDOBOOKS.COM
Published by Abdo Publishing, a division of ABDO, PO Box 398166, Minneapolis, Minnesota 55439.

Printed in China.
052025
092025

THIS BOOK CONTAINS RECYCLED MATERIALS

Cover Photos: Michal Krakowiak/E+/Getty Images (main); Shutterstock Images (pattern)
Interior Photos: Shutterstock Images, 4–5, 9, 10, 14–15, 18 (globe), 22, 26, 27, 28, 30–31, 37, 40–41, 42–43, 44, 50, 56, 60, 71, 76–77, 78, 86, 88–89, 93, 94, 98, 101; Rudmer Zwerver/Shutterstock Images, 6; Eric Isselee/Shutterstock Images, 7; Ondrej Bucek/Shutterstock Images, 16–17; Red Line Editorial, 18 (map); Wolf Avni/Shutterstock Images, 20–21; Nadine Klose/Shutterstock Images, 25; Gabriella Shipman/Shutterstock Images, 32; Cormac Price/Shutterstock Images, 34; Simon Eeman/Shutterstock Images, 35; Hesti Lestari/Shutterstock Images, 38; Abraham Badenhorst/Shutterstock Images, 45; powerofforever/DigitalVision Vectors/Getty Images, 46; Oistein Thomassen/Alamy, 52; Goddard_Photography/iStock Unreleased/Getty Images, 53; Subodh Agnihotri/iStockphoto, 54–55; Kathy Hutchins/Shutterstock Images, 59; Peter Rhys Williams/Shutterstock Images, 63; Thegift777/iStock Unreleased/Getty Images, 64; iStockphoto, 65, 79; Felix Lipov/Shutterstock Images, 66–67; Arnold Petersen/Shutterstock Images, 72; Jurie Maree/Shutterstock Images, 74; Andrew Hagen/Shutterstock Images, 81; Fokke Baarssen/Shutterstock Images, 82; Old Mill Photography/Shutterstock Images, 91; Wesley Lazarus/Shutterstock Images, 95

Editor: Kari Cornell
Series Designer: Maggie Villaume

Library of Congress Control Number: 2024948574

PUBLISHER'S CATALOGING-IN-PUBLICATION DATA
Names: Edwards, Sue Bradford, author.
Title: South Africa / by Sue Bradford Edwards
Description: Minneapolis, Minnesota: Abdo Publishing, 2026 | Series: Essential library of countries | Includes online resources and index.
Identifiers: ISBN 9781098297015 (lib. bdg.) | ISBN 9798384919537 (ebook)
Subjects: LCSH: Geography--Juvenile literature. | South Africa--Juvenile literature. | Africa--Juvenile literature. | South Africa--History--Juvenile literature.
Classification: DDC 968--dc23

CONTENTS

CHAPTER **ONE**

A TOUR OF SOUTH AFRICA

Aunt Meg placed a bowl of thick porridge in front of Charlotte and her brother, Marcus. "This is called *mealie pap*," she said. "It's made of corn flour with some milk and sugar added." Charlotte and Marcus had arrived in Johannesburg, South Africa, the night before to visit their aunt and uncle. The four gathered at the breakfast table to start their first day of exploration.

"It's fantastic," Charlotte said. She could tell Marcus agreed by how quickly he spooned the creamy mixture into his mouth. "What are we going to do today?"

"Well, since you both love animals, we've decided our first stop should be Kruger National Park," Uncle Jeff said. "Be sure to grab your jackets, though. July may

The city of Johannesburg was founded in 1886 after gold was discovered nearby. It became known as "the city of gold."

Kruger National Park is home to African elephants, which can live as long as 70 years.

be summertime in the United States, but we're in the Southern Hemisphere, so the seasons are reversed. That means we're in the middle of winter."

ANIMALS IN THE WILD

Charlotte and Marcus knew Kruger National Park was a place where animals roamed safely in the wide-open spaces of their natural habitats. It was a five-hour drive to the park, and the siblings watched the countryside shift from city to farmland to a landscape of trees and hills. When the family stopped for lunch, Charlotte got her first taste of *vetkoek*, small balls of fried dough topped with curried beef and cheese. Her uncle explained that vetkoek meant "fat cake" in Afrikaans, one of the 12 official languages spoken in South Africa.[1]

Once they arrived at Kruger's Malelane Gate, the family climbed aboard an open-air truck with other tourists and ventured into the park. Soon the truck was bouncing along dirt trails. "Look, zebras!" Charlotte called out as she saw a herd grazing on a large, grassy plain.

"I see a Cape buffalo," Marcus said as he pointed at the huge animal drinking from a pond. Then their guide told them to look up as a martial eagle, South Africa's biggest eagle, flew overhead and landed in a nearby tree. By the end of the day, the family had seen elephants spraying each other with water from a pond, and they had even seen a pride of lions lazing in the tall grass.

PROTECTING SOUTH AFRICA'S ANIMALS

In 1884, Paul Kruger, the president of a former province of South Africa called the Transvaal, realized the area's wild animals needed protection, so he restricted hunting in part of the Transvaal. In 1898, the area was expanded into Sabie Game Reserve. Today the park, which was renamed Kruger National Park in 1927, covers 7,580 square miles (19,633 sq km) and is home to more than 750 animal species and 1,980 different kinds of plants.[2] Hunting is prohibited in the park, and the only shots tourists can take are with a camera.

LEARNING ABOUT APARTHEID

The family stayed overnight in a lodge near the park. Marcus was surprised they could see elephants and giraffes from their rooms. In the morning, they drove back to Johannesburg.

The next day, they visited the Apartheid Museum. Back home in the United States, Charlotte and Marcus had learned about apartheid.

They knew that it was a system of laws designed to keep people of different races apart. This system favored white people and discriminated against people of color.

At the museum, they came face-to-face with how apartheid had affected all areas of life in South Africa. Charlotte and Uncle Jeff received entry tickets that said "non-white," but Marcus's and Aunt Meg's tickets said "white." They entered through the appropriate doors, following two separate corridors that met up before the exhibits. After talking it over, Charlotte and her brother realized that although she had to climb stairs, he had entered up a gradual ramp that was easy to climb. He had no idea Charlotte had to walk up steps. The museum was open to all, but separate entrances showed visitors the everyday reality of life under apartheid. They learned that from 1948 through the 1990s, many public buildings in South Africa had separate entrances.

As they walked through the museum and studied the exhibits, Marcus was upset by how badly people of color had been treated under apartheid. He didn't think it was fair that white people had so many advantages. As they left, Charlotte said, "I can tell Nelson Mandela was very important in the fight against apartheid, but I'd like to learn more about him."

"Perfect, because that's exactly what we're going to do next," Uncle Jeff said.

MANDELA HOUSE AND SOWETO

The family stopped for lunch at Kwa Mai Mai market. The neighborhood was full of street vendors selling tasty food. They shared a huge plate of barbecued beef and sausages, with fresh tomatoes on the side.

The Apartheid Museum opened in 2001 with a mission to chronicle the rise and fall of the apartheid system in South Africa.

Soweto was developed as a place for Black South Africans to live in the 1930s. It is home to approximately 1.9 million people.

Afterward, they drove to a township called Soweto, short for "South Western Townships." Uncle Jeff explained that the government had created the township in the 1930s when it forced Black people to live in an area separate from white people. Charlotte had gotten used to the modern apartment buildings and houses in other parts of Johannesburg. These homes were small and crammed together, and many had tin roofs. Aunt Meg mentioned that in the townships, some homes don't have electricity or running water.

The family decided to go on a walking tour, so Uncle Jeff led them to a group of bamboo huts with thatched roofs to meet their guide. Charlotte and Marcus listened intently as their guide explained what life was like in Soweto during apartheid. Marcus was especially interested in the Hector Pieterson Memorial, which told the story of the Soweto student uprising against apartheid in 1976. Twelve-year-old Hector was one of the students killed by police, and he became a symbol of the fight.

Charlotte's favorite part was their visit to the Mandela House, the small home where Nelson Mandela lived from 1946 until his arrest in 1962. A quote from Mandela in the home read, "The bedroom was so small that a double bed took up almost the entire floor space." Displays told the story of Mandela's struggles and triumphs. Charlotte couldn't believe that Mandela had spent 27 years in prison, and that in 1988, while he was away, the house burned down but was rebuilt by neighbors. Mandela returned to the home when he was released from prison in 1990, and it was declared a public heritage site in 1999.

CAPE TOWN GOVERNMENT

The family spent a few days back in Johannesburg. Then they drove to the airport and flew to Cape Town on the country's southern tip. "I didn't realize South Africa was so big," Charlotte commented as they got off the plane and found their rental car.

Cape Town is about 868 miles (1,397 km) from Johannesburg by road.[3]

"I can smell the salty air, so we must be near the sea," Marcus said. Charlotte nodded. She was staring at a large mountain looming over the city.

"We'll be exploring the sea and the mountain tomorrow," Aunt Meg promised. "Cape Town has wonderful restaurants. What do you think about some *braai*, traditional South African barbecue?"

All agreed that sounded delicious, so they found a place to feast on grilled lamb chops and lobster tails.

After lunch, they walked to a large group of buildings with South African flags flying in front. "These are the Houses of Parliament. This is one of the places where government officials meet," Uncle Jeff explained.

Marcus and Charlotte were surprised to learn that South Africa has three different capitals. Only the legislative part of the government, where laws are made, is in Cape Town. As they toured the building, built in 1885, they learned that South Africa's government was very similar to the government in the United States because it was divided into three parts, called the executive, legislative, and judicial branches. They even stood in the room where Mandela had addressed parliament after he became president in 1994.

Table Mountain is 3,560 feet (1,085 m) tall.[4]

BEAUTIFUL NATURE

The next day, the family went to Table Mountain. It took two hours to make the strenuous climb up the steep sides, following a path that included staircases made of rocks and views of scrubby trees and tall grass on the mountain's side. "Amazing!" Marcus said as they reached the mountain's flat top and could see the bright blue waters of the Atlantic Ocean. He looked out across the flat, table-like top of the mountain. "I can see how this mountain got its name," he added.

"It's called a plateau, an area of flat land," Uncle Jeff explained. "But its original name is Hoerikwaggo. This is a Khoisan word meaning 'Mountain in the Sea.'"

The family enjoyed a picnic lunch of cold meats and salads as they gazed out at the view from the top. Then they took a cable car ride back down to the bottom. The car swayed in the breeze, and Charlotte held on tight as they traveled down the mountain suspended from a thick wire. They drove a short distance, leaving behind open countryside and driving past homes and businesses before they reached Boulders Beach. As they stepped onto the sand, Charlotte was amazed to see penguins right there on the beach.

Aunt Meg explained that the birds were African penguins, and they had been in South Africa since 1983, when they migrated from a nearby island. Tourists could get close to take photos because the birds were used to people, but visitors were not allowed to touch the endangered birds. Charlotte could have stayed until dinner, but there was one more adventure in store for them that day.

Their next stop brought them right to the ocean at the Cape of Good Hope. As the wind whipped back her hair, Charlotte read a sign announcing this was the most

PORTUGAL'S CONNECTION TO THE CAPE OF GOOD HOPE

The first European to visit the Cape of Good Hope was a Portuguese explorer named Bartolomeu Dias. Portuguese explorers had sailed down the coast of Africa, leaving stone markers to indicate how far they had traveled. In 1488, Dias sailed around the cape. His journey proved that the Atlantic and Indian Oceans were linked and that sailing to India from Europe was possible. Ten years later, another Portuguese explorer, Vasco da Gama, became the first European to reach India by sailing around the cape.

More than 800,000 visitors come to Table Mountain each year, and many take photos. It is South Africa's most popular landmark to photograph.

southwestern point of the African continent. "What a rugged place!" Marcus shouted to be heard above the crashing waves that slammed against the rocks below. The family followed a path downward and wandered the shore as Charlotte thought about how much there was to see, do, and learn in South Africa.

A COMPLICATED HISTORY

The story of South Africa stretches back thousands of years to when early humans lived in the region. Since then, people from many different cultures have made their homes there. When European settlers arrived, they forced the local people into a segregated society in which they had few rights, while the minority white population enjoyed wealth, privilege, and power.

A stronger nation emerged from the struggle for equality, but South Africa still faces many challenges. The country is finding its place in the world and attracting tourists with its stunning deserts, mountains, forests, ocean waters, and unique animal and plant species. The nation's natural beauty, tumultuous history, and diverse cultures make South Africa a fascinating place to visit.

CHAPTER **TWO**

GEOGRAPHY

South Africa consists of 470,693 square miles (1,219,090 sq km) of total area at the southern tip of the African continent.[1] It is located in the Southern Hemisphere, or the southern half of Earth. It is bordered by the countries of Eswatini, Mozambique, and Zimbabwe to the northeast. Botswana and Namibia lie to the north. Lesotho is located in the southeast, completely encircled by South Africa. South Africa is divided into nine provinces: the Western Cape, Eastern Cape, Northern Cape, KwaZulu-Natal, Free State, Mpumalanga, Gauteng, North West, and Limpopo.

South Africa is a fairly dry country with an average annual rainfall of approximately 18 inches (46 cm).[2] The westernmost province, the Western Cape, gets most of its rain in the winter. For the rest of the nation, the majority of the rain falls in the summer.

The Drakensberg mountains are one of four mountain ranges that form South Africa's Great Escarpment, which divides the coastal plains from inland plateaus.

MAP OF SOUTH AFRICA

KEY:
- Capital
- City
- Point of Interest

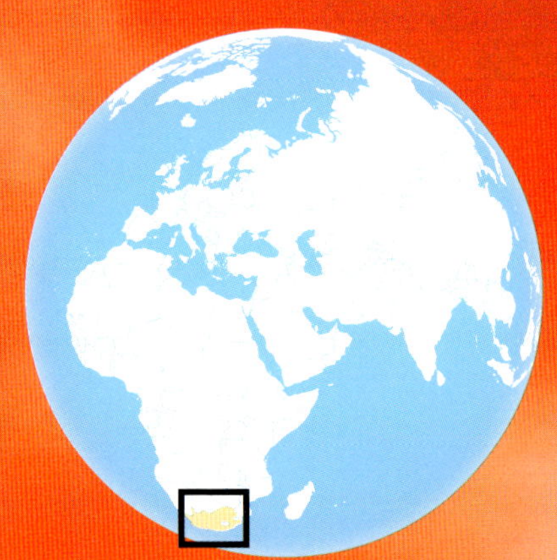

South Africa is subtropical, meaning it is somewhat cooler and drier than the tropical regions that lie to the north. This is because it is farther from the equator than tropical regions and because it is surrounded on three sides by the Atlantic Ocean and the Indian Ocean. Winds blow from the west to the east, carrying cool Atlantic air across the country. Polar air also moves across the nation in the winter, bringing colder temperatures as well as rain and snow.

Temperatures in South Africa vary according to the season. Summers can be hot, with daytime temperatures of 70 to 90 degrees Fahrenheit (21–32°C).[3] Winters are much cooler, but the temperature varies from one location to another within the country. This is because the nation is composed of three geographic regions—the plateau, mountains known as the Great Escarpment, and the land between the Great Escarpment and the ocean.

SOUTH AFRICAN SEASONS

Earth rotates on its axis, an imaginary line extending from the North Pole to the South Pole. Earth is tilted on its axis. In June the Northern Hemisphere is tilted toward the sun and gets more direct rays. The Southern Hemisphere gets less direct sunlight. June is summer in the Northern Hemisphere. In the Southern Hemisphere, including South Africa, June is winter.

THE PLATEAU

Much of South Africa is covered by a high plateau. The plateau is almost completely made of ancient rock that formed between the Late Carboniferous Epoch (about 359 to 300 million years ago) and the Late Triassic Epoch (about 230 to 200 million years ago). The plateau is highest in the east, where it reaches more than 8,000 feet (2,400 m) above sea level in the area near Lesotho. In the Kalahari Desert in the west, the elevation is approximately 2,000 feet (600 m).[4]

The central part of the plateau consists of grasslands, an area known as the highveld. *Veld* means "grassland" in Afrikaans. The rolling grasslands here lie between 4,000 and 6,000 feet (1,200 and 1,800 m) in elevation.[5] Much of the area that was traditionally covered by open grassland is now agricultural land, but there are still undisturbed pockets of natural vegetation for visitors to see. The highveld extends from the northeastern corner of Western Cape Province across all of the Free State Province.

In the north, the highveld rises into rock formations called the Witwatersrand, or Rand. The Rand is composed of gold-bearing rock and is approximately 62 miles (100 km) by 23 miles (37 km).[6] The Rand is also home to the country's largest city, Johannesburg.

North of the Rand is the bushveld. This grassland is dotted with trees and occurs between 3,300 and 4,900 feet (1,000 and 1,500 m) in elevation.[7] This region is composed of volcanic rock that contains the minerals platinum, chromium, copper, fluorspar, gold, nickel, and iron. The bushveld is in Gauteng, North West, and Eastern Cape Provinces. It is famous for its wildlife, which includes wildebeests and buffalo.

Much of the Free State in north-central South Africa is part of the highveld.

The rolling red earth hills of the Kalahari Desert edge into South Africa's North West and Northern Cape provinces.

The Kalahari Desert is located within the plateau region of southern Africa, extending into the north-central part of South Africa. The desert is a gently rolling, sand-covered plain at a minimum of 3,000 feet (900 m) above sea level.[8] It is not entirely arid. Parts of the South African Kalahari have more water and support plants, making the area home to a variety of wildlife, including cheetahs and lions.

WATER: A CRITICAL RESOURCE

South Africa's population continues to grow. This poses a problem when it comes to drinking and household water, especially in a nation where less than 45 percent of the population has water piped into their homes.[10] Contamination of water sources by the mining industry makes getting clean water more difficult. BN Aqua Solutions built a processing plant to purify acidic water left over from mining and make it safe for drinking and agriculture.

THE GREAT ESCARPMENT

A semicircle of mountains roughly parallel to the South African coastline borders the highveld to the east, south, and west of the plateau. These mountains consist of several ranges and are known as the Great Escarpment. They separate the plateau from a narrow strip of land along the South African coast.

The majority of these mountain ranges formed when water eroded away parts of the land that had been uplifted by volcanic activity. Headwaters of several rivers formed along the escarpment's edge. In the mountains, nighttime winter temperatures can drop below freezing. In the day, temperatures can rise to 50 to 70 degrees Fahrenheit (10–21°C).[9]

At 11,320 feet (3,450 m), Mafadi Peak in the Drakensberg mountains is the highest point in South Africa.[14]

The Drakensberg mountains are the largest and most dramatic of these mountain ranges. The range stretches from Eastern Cape Province to Eswatini. The Drakensberg mountains reach elevations of more than 11,400 feet (3,475 m), and the range extends from South Africa's northeast to the southwest for 700 miles (1,126 km), running parallel to the nation's southeastern coast.[11]

The Drakensberg range consists of eroded basalt, a volcanic rock, on a base of sandstone. Sandstone is a sedimentary rock composed of sediment, or sand, that mixed with clay and later formed rock. The Drakensberg range's steep eastern slope ranges in elevation from 10,000 feet (3,000 m) to more than 11,000 feet (3,300 m) between Lesotho and KwaZulu-Natal Province.[12]

The local Zulu, a South African ethnic group, call the eastern Drakensberg range *Quathlamba*, which means "barrier of pointed spears" or "piled-up rocks." The southern slope of the Drakensberg range is 7,900 feet to 10,000 feet (2,400 to 3,000 m) in elevation and extends between Lesotho and Eastern Cape Province.[13] Below the southern and eastern slopes of the Drakensberg mountains are sandstone terraces where outcrops of basalt jut into the air. Deep valleys run from this area to the ocean.

In the western and southwestern areas of the Great Escarpment are the Cape Ranges, a group of fold mountains. They formed because Earth's surface is covered by massive tectonic plates that shift. When one tectonic plate pushes another, sometimes one plate folds, much like the wrinkles

The basalt rock formations of the Drakensberg mountains are protected in Royal Natal National Park. The formation left of center is called Policeman's Helmet.

that form when someone pushes up their sleeve. The Cape Ranges were formed by this type of fold, forming an L where north-south ranges meet east-west ranges. The north-south Cape Ranges run parallel to the Atlantic coastline. They include the Cederberg Mountains, the Witzenberg Mountains, and the Groot Winterhoek Mountains, which all have peaks more than 6,600 feet

(2,000 m) in elevation. The east-west ranges are parallel to the southern coastline and include the Swartberg Mountains and the Langeberg Mountains. The highest of these peaks are more than 7,200 feet (2,200 m) in elevation.[15]

BEACHES AND COASTLINE

The narrow coastal strip between the Great Escarpment and the ocean is called the lowveld, and it varies in width from about 37 miles (60 km) to more than 124 miles (200 km).[16] On the coast, winter temperatures are generally warmest in the east and coolest in the west. Off the South African coastline is the continental shelf, the area of the seabed around the continent of Africa where the ocean is shallow compared with the deep, open ocean. This seabed is narrow in the west but grows wider in the south, where deposits of oil and natural gas that can be used for energy have been found.

About halfway between the coast of South Africa and Antarctica are the Prince Edward Islands.

LANDLOCKED LESOTHO

Within the Drakensberg mountains in eastern South Africa is the Kingdom of Lesotho. It is 11,720 square miles (30,355 sq km) in size, and two-thirds of the country is covered by mountains.[17] It is considered landlocked because it has no coastline and is instead surrounded by land. Much of South Africa's water comes from the snowcapped peaks of this country. Lesotho uses its fast-flowing rivers to produce electricity, and the country sells both power and water to South Africa.

African penguins are the main attraction at Boulders Beach in Simon's Town, Western Cape Province. About 60,000 visitors come each year to see the aquatic birds, which have inhabited the area since 1983.

The Orange River plunges 184 feet (56 m) over the highest point of Augrabies Falls in Augrabies Falls National Park.

The two islands, Prince Edward Island and Marion Island, are volcanic peaks. They were claimed by South Africa in 1947 and are largely uninhabited. They have an average temperature of 40 degrees Fahrenheit (4.4°C) and 100 inches (250 cm) of yearly precipitation.[18] A ship visits Marion Island each April to bring scientists who work at the weather observatory and study the ocean and animal life.

RIVERS AND LAKES

Water is a precious resource in South Africa. There are no large natural lakes, so large artificial lakes were created primarily to irrigate crops. None of the country's rivers are large enough to be navigable by ships, and sand that washed down to the river mouths makes these areas too shallow to be used as harbors.

The largest river in South Africa is the Orange River, which is 1,300 miles (2,100 km) long. It flows from the Drakensberg mountains in Lesotho west to the Atlantic Ocean. It is joined by its major tributary, the smaller Vaal River, and together they form a drainage basin of approximately 330,000 square miles (854,000 sq km).[19] These rivers are important sources of water for agriculture, urban areas, and industry.

The Breede River is another South African river. At 199 miles (320 km) long, it is the longest navigable river in Western Cape Province.[20] It provides water to irrigate orchards and vineyards and is a popular destination for fishing and kayaking.

Another major river, flowing through both South Africa and Mozambique, is the Limpopo, which is 1,100 miles (1,800 km) long.[21] It begins in northeastern South Africa at the point where the Crocodile and Marico Rivers join together. This river forms part of the border between South Africa and the neighboring countries of Botswana and Zimbabwe before flowing into Mozambique.

CHAPTER **THREE**

PLANTS AND ANIMALS

Tourists who come to South Africa to go on a safari are led through wild areas by guides in the hope that they will get to see the country's wildlife. Sometimes tourists spot patrolling rangers who protect animals from poachers. Poachers are people who want to illegally hunt and kill protected animals.

People on a safari often want to photograph the Big Five, five famous African animals that can all be found in Kruger National Park. The African bush elephant is the largest land animal on the planet and can weigh as much as 7.7 short tons (7 metric tons). Elephants are big eaters, with each animal consuming up to 600 pounds (270 kg) of grass, leaves, and tree shoots each day. They travel in herds of up to ten females and their calves.[1]

South Africa's Kruger National Park is a popular safari destination. The best time to see animals there is between May and October.

Lions are territorial, living in and protecting the same area for many years.

Tourists also want to see lions. Male lions are larger than females, standing up to four feet (1.2 m) tall at the shoulders and weighing more than 440 pounds (200 kg). Lions live in family groups called prides. Each pride consists of as many as 12 females and their young along with the pride's males. The number of males varies between two and six.[2]

Lions generally hunt at night, preying on large animals including zebras, wildebeests, buffalo, gemsbok antelope, and even giraffes. The females tend to do most of the hunting, working together in packs to bring down prey. Living and hunting in prides helps lions survive.

Leopards are golden cats speckled with dark spots. The second-largest African cats, they weigh anywhere from 44 to 198 pounds (20 to 90 kg).[3] Leopards primarily hunt at night, preying mainly on medium and small antelope. They also hunt baboons, foxes, fish, reptiles, and hyraxes, which are small mammals that look like guinea pigs but are related to elephants. Having a wide range of prey makes it easier for this solo hunter to find food.

Another impressive sight is the rhinoceros, or rhino. This herbivore lives on a diet of plants, including fruits, twigs, stems, grasses, and leaves. The black rhino has two horns and lives in thickets and densely growing brush. The two-horned white rhino is found most often in woodlands. The two species vary in size, with the smaller black rhino ranging from 1,760 to 2,650 pounds (800 to 1,200 kg). White rhinos weigh from 3,970 to 4,410 pounds (1,800 to 2,000 kg).[4]

The African or Cape buffalo weighs up to 1,650 pounds (750 kg) and is five feet (1.5 m) tall at the shoulder.[5] Adults are dark gray to black, while youngsters are reddish brown in color. Males and females both have heavy ridged horns. The males use their horns to show dominance. The buffalo live in herds of several hundred animals and can be found both in woodlands and on grasslands. Herd life brings protection from predators.

BUILT FOR SPEED

A hunting cheetah can sprint at 75 miles per hour (120 kmh), making it the fastest land animal on Earth. Its long tail allows it to balance and quickly change direction at these speeds to go after a dodging antelope. Cheetahs have big lungs, which help them take 150 breaths a minute, giving these cats enough oxygen to fuel the chase.[7] Cheetahs also have longer legs than other cats, which lengthens their stride. All of these attributes make for a fast-moving hunter.

STILL MORE ANIMALS

In addition to the Big Five, there are many other animals in South Africa. One of the most easily recognized is the ostrich. The largest bird in the world, it is up to 9 feet (2.7 m) tall.[6] Because it does not fly, its feathers have adapted to keep it cool. The ostrich can hold its feathers away from its body to form a layer of insulating air. Ostriches mate for life, and both mates help raise their young.

Two species of zebras live in South Africa. Cape mountain zebras, which live in the rocky uplands, almost went extinct in the 1930s. The Burchell's zebra, a plains zebra, is common throughout the highveld. It has adapted to easily digest any grass it finds with the help of the bacteria that live in its digestive tract.

Another grazing animal is the Cape giraffe, which lives in the highveld and forest lands. It feeds on leaves, flowers, fruits, and shoots of woody plants. This includes the tall African acacia tree, which is easily recognized by its flat top. Just as the giraffe adapted to reach the leaves of trees, the acacia's shape is an adaptation to arid South African winds, which pass across the treetop without drying out the tightly clustered leaves.

Many different antelope species make South Africa their home. Blue wildebeests can be found

DEADLY SNAKES

Between 130 and 160 snake species live in South Africa. The most feared is the black mamba, which is venomous. A venomous snake kills its prey by biting it and injecting it with venom. A black mamba can be 15 feet (4.5 m) long and reach speeds of 12 miles per hour (20 kmh). The snake is generally olive to dark brown in color with the black coloration limited to the inside of its mouth. It lives in the grasses and brush of the North West, Limpopo, Mpumalanga, and northern KwaZulu-Natal Provinces.[8]

Blue wildebeests stand about five feet (1.5 m) tall and can weigh up to 600 pounds (272 kg).

roaming the countryside in herds numbering from ten animals to several thousand. They are silver gray with dark manes and hooked horns. Migrations are more limited than in the past because of agricultural fencing.

Unlike the many antelope that live in vast herds, the steenbok lives alone or in mated pairs on the grasslands. It has evolved to not need drinking water. It survives drought by getting water from its food.

The most common tortoise in South Africa is the leopard tortoise, which lives in most parts of the country except the highveld. These tortoises are approximately two and a half feet (76 cm) long.[9] They eat grasses and succulents and even gnaw on bones and hyena feces.

Both brown and spotted hyenas live in South Africa. They often hunt in packs, going after larger animals. Lone hyenas will hunt smaller prey and scavenge for food. A pack of hyenas can bring down a zebra or buffalo.

The hippopotamus, or hippo, lives in and near rivers. It weighs up to approximately 2.8 short tons (2.5 metric tons).[10] At night it grazes along the riverbank, eating grasses and drinking water. One of the few animals that is a threat to the hippo is the crocodile, which reaches 18 feet (5.5 m) in length. Although 70 percent of the crocodile's diet is fish, it will also eat a hippo, wildebeest, or zebra. Having a diverse diet helps the crocodile survive at times of the year when one food source is scarce.[11]

South Africa has nearly 300 mammal species, approximately 860 bird species, and about 8,000 plant species.[12]

UNIQUE PLANTS

Just as South Africa is home to many unique animals, it is also home to diverse plants, including palm trees with frond-like leaves. The lala or molala palm tree reaches 16 to 23 feet (5–7 m) tall. Each tree produces up to 2,000 round, orangish fruits that taste like gingerbread and take up to two years to ripen and another two years to fall from the plant.[13] Elephants, monkeys, and baboons eat these fruits.

Another palm tree is the wild date palm, which reaches approximately 20 feet (6 m) tall.[14] It requires a steady supply of water, so its presence is one indicator that an area has reliable water sources. Its fruits are eaten by birds and people, but people also eat the center of the tree, called a palm heart.

Another unique South African plant is in danger of going extinct. The Clanwilliam cedar

The Clanwilliam cedar dates back 225 million years and has become one of the rarest trees on Earth.

is found in the Cederberg mountains north of Cape Town. Now a rare sight, the tree was once so common that Cederberg is named after it. Because the wood has an attractive appearance, is durable, and even smells good, these trees were lumbered to near extinction.

Most Clanwilliam cedars reach about 16 feet (5 m) tall, but in protected areas they may grow to 66 feet (20 m).[15] The tree is a conifer, producing both tiny male cones and spherical female cones that take up to three years to mature and drop seeds. Because the area where they grow is prone to drought, wildfire is also a threat.

Sugarbushes, or African proteas, are found only in South Africa. Although many are small, the largest sugarbush varieties reach 25 feet (8 m) tall.[16] Some have leathery, oval-shaped leaves, while others have pine needle–shaped leaves. Leaves range in color from light green to dark blue green, and the flowers often look like pincushions or fireworks of pink, red, white, or yellow. The plants are pollinated by a wide variety of animals, from nectar-feeding sugarbirds and sunbirds to insects and even rodents. Gerbils, mice, rats, and shrews all feed on the nectar and help with pollination.

SOUTH AFRICA'S NATIONAL FLOWER

The king protea is also known as the giant protea, honeypot, or king sugarbush. It is South Africa's national flower. It has the largest flower head of any protea. When fully opened, the flower looks much like a crown perched among the plant's leaves. It looks like a large pink flower with a white center, but the outer pink petals are actually bracts, or modified leaves, that surround the true blossoms, a cluster of yellow and red petals in the center.

Brush fires are a common occurrence in South Africa, and some sugarbushes grow among rocks, where fire is unlikely to spread. Others are stimulated by fire to quickly grow new stems, and there are some that have seed pods that open to release the seeds only after being in the heat of a fire. There are 360 protea species. Approximately 120 are endangered due to habitat loss and overcollection by people who want to sell them or grow them at home.[17]

MARINE LIFE

Some tourists come to South Africa for its marine wildlife, which includes southern right whales, so named because whalers considered them the right whale to hunt. Today these ocean mammals are tracked by scientists and nature lovers who identify individual whales by the patterns of calluses on their heads. The playful whales sometimes breach, breaking the ocean's surface. They are up to 52 feet (16 m) long and weigh as much as 70 short tons (64 metric tons).[18] Right whales migrate from their feeding grounds in Antarctica, arriving at the coast during the South African winter.

Another dramatic marine animal is the great white shark. This hunter consumes dolphins, seals, birds, and fish. It can be more than 20 feet (6 m) long and can weigh up to 2.8 short tons (2.5 metric tons).[19] Great white sharks have large gill slits, openings that enable water to pass over their gills. This provides the sharks with the oxygen they need to chase their prey.

Bottlenose dolphins are frequent visitors to the South African coast. They travel in pods of five to 15 animals, although superpods of 600 dolphins have been spotted.[20] They are often seen swimming in the wake left behind a fast-moving boat.

Right whales can be seen along the coast between Cape Town and Durban during the month of June.

Cape fur seals live along South Africa's west coast, where they spend at least 30 percent of their time in the water. Their large eyes help them see underwater to hunt fish and avoid great white sharks. They can dive to depths of more than 1,310 feet (400 m) and stay underwater for up to ten minutes.[21] Many other fish and aquatic animals are found in the ocean around South Africa. These include species that people keep in aquariums, such as seahorses, puffer fish, and gobies. There are also rays that silently glide through the sea.

CHAPTER **FOUR**

HISTORY

Many peoples have made South Africa their home, including early human ancestors. This is why an area located 30 miles (50 km) from Johannesburg is called the Cradle of Humankind.[1] In 1924, this was where scientists found the fossilized skull of *Australopithecus africanus*, an extinct hominin that lived more than three million years ago. *Hominin* is the scientific term for modern humans and their non-ape ancestors.

Remains belonging to *Australopithecus africanus* weren't the only fossils in the area. In 2015, scientists found more than 1,500 human fossils in the Rising Star caves.[2] From the size and shape of the bones, scientists knew they had found a new hominin species. They estimated it lived 335,000 to 236,000 years ago

Paleontologists began to excavate fossils of human ancestors from Sterkfontein caves in 1936. Some of the fossils are believed to be almost two million years old.

alongside modern humans, or *Homo sapiens*. They named the new species *Homo naledi*.

One of the earliest human groups to live in what is now South Africa was a group of hunter-gatherers called the San, who have lived in the area for at least 20,000 years. Hunter-gatherers hunt animals and gather wild plant foods. The San lived in the Kalahari Desert. Scientists from the University of Pennsylvania studied the DNA of modern African peoples including the San, a group that still lives in South Africa. In 2009, the scientists announced that DNA evidence showed the San are descended from South Africa's earliest humans.

The Khoikhoi arrived in South Africa about 2,000 years ago. They were pastoralists, who originally herded sheep and later cattle to trade with Europeans. They followed their herds from one fresh pasture to another, living in oval huts covered in reed mats. As many as 100 huts were arranged in villages called kraals.[3]

The first farming people arrived in the area surrounding the Limpopo River approximately 1,800 years ago. Coming from West Africa, they were ancestors of modern people who speak

SAN ROCK ART

Evidence of early San peoples can be hard to find since they didn't build villages. But they did paint. The San created between 35,000 and 40,000 paintings in caves and rock overhangs in the Drakensberg mountains. Their paintings show hunters pursuing eland and rhebok antelope. Paints were made from burned bone, charcoal, iron oxide or rust, white clay, and even bird droppings, each of which was mixed with blood and fat to make different colors. Some of this rock art is 8,000 years old.[4]

Bantu languages. They built villages and used iron tools to clear the land and plant melons, gourds, legumes, and the grains millet and sorghum. Starting 1,500 years ago, they also kept cattle.

EUROPEAN ARRIVAL

The San, Khoikhoi, and early farmers were living in South Africa when the Portuguese began exploring the continent's western coast in search of a sea route to India and the riches of the spice trade. In early 1488, Bartolomeu Dias became the first European to sail around the southern tip of Africa. Portugal dominated this sea route but was uninterested in settling the area. The Portuguese focused on gold and silver from Africa's interior and the trade of enslaved people from the Kongo region on Africa's central west coast.

By the early 1600s, the British and Dutch had journeyed to South Africa as well. Cape Town was

A statue of Bartolomeu Dias stands in Cape Town. One account states that Dias originally named the area the Cape of Storms, but it was later renamed Cape of Good Hope by King John II of Portugal to attract more settlers.

The Boers fought fiercely against the British to defend their farms and their way of life, which included slavery, a practice the British wanted to end.

founded by the Dutch East India Company (VOC) in 1652 to provide fresh fruits, vegetables, and meat to Dutch ships sailing to Asia. The location was chosen because there was fresh water in the area, which is why the Khoikhoi grazed their herds there. Although the VOC forbade enslavement of the Khoikhoi, Dutch farmers immigrating to the area brought enslaved peoples from West and East Africa, India, and Southeast Asia's Malay Peninsula. By 1700, the settlement was growing wheat and wine grapes and herding sheep and cattle.

As the VOC developed the area around Cape Town, Dutch pastoralists called Boers immigrated to the area. By 1800, the Boers had taken land occupied by the early Bantu-speaking farmers, splitting South Africa. The Boers controlled the west and the Bantu-speaking people controlled the eastern highveld.

Britain annexed the area that they called the Cape Colony in 1806, making it part of the British Empire. The colony extended along the entire southernmost tip of what would become South Africa. In 1807, the British abolished enslavement. At the time, Boer farmers were forcing San and Khoikhoi people to work for them.

The Boer farmers relied on this forced labor to run their farms. When the British proclaimed an end to slavery in the Cape Colony, the Boers left the area. From 1835 to 1845, 12,000 to 14,000 Boers and their allies immigrated north of the Orange River, slaughtering many Ndebele people, a Bantu-speaking people who had lived in the region since the 1700s.[5] The Boers farmed this land, continuing to use forced labor.

Surviving Ndebele people were driven to Zimbabwe. In 1852, this area became the Orange Free State and the Transvaal. This left the Boers in control of the interior highveld and the British in control of much of the rest of modern South Africa. As the Boers colonized this area, they added some Bantu vocabulary from the local Zulu people to their Dutch language, leading to the development of a hybrid language called Afrikaans.

By 1707, 1,779 settlers and 1,107 enslaved people lived in the Cape Town area.[6]

The British wanted to control the Orange Free State and the Transvaal, which the Boers had claimed as their own. The Boers wanted to be independent from Britain. This led to the Boer War (1899–1902), in which 500,000 British soldiers battled 88,000 Boers. The Boers used guerrilla tactics, striking and then running. The British burned Boer and African farms. They also captured and imprisoned people in segregated camps, where an estimated 26,000 Boer women and children died.[7] Eventually the British won.

THE BIRTH OF SOUTH AFRICA

The British Parliament passed the South Africa Act of 1909, creating the Union of South Africa. The boundaries were the same as the modern nation. Only white delegates representing the white population, which made up less than 20 percent of the total population, had a role in the process.[8] The Union of South Africa was part of the British Empire. Power was concentrated in an all-white Parliament.

THE RISE OF THE AFRICAN NATIONAL CONGRESS

An organization called the South African Native National Congress, founded in 1912, worked for the rights of Black and Coloured South Africans. In 1923, it was renamed the African National Congress (ANC), and in the 1940s the organization shifted its focus to abolishing apartheid. In 1960, when the white South African government banned the ANC, it functioned in exile until the ban was lifted in 1990. In 1994, Nelson Mandela, president of the ANC, became the head of South Africa's first multiethnic government.

Dutch Afrikaners held power and dominated the Black African majority. The new nation's constitution kept Black people from voting and running for office, and laws segregated housing, land ownership, and jobs. Eventually Black South Africans were forced to live in urban slums or on white-owned farms where they also worked. In 1931, the British Parliament passed the Statute of Westminster, making independent countries of South Africa, Canada, Australia, New Zealand, and Ireland. White South Africans continued to hold power.

During World War II (1939–1945), factories were built in South African cities and industry boomed. Black South Africans moved to the cities to work, forming trade unions, a type of worker's association that demanded higher pay and more rights for workers. In 1948, the pro-white National Party swept the South African elections and announced apartheid, a program that reinforced segregation and discrimination. It divided the South African people by race—white, Black, Indian, Asian, and Coloured, or mixed-race. Laws forced people apart. People from different racial groups had to live separately and were forbidden from intermarrying. Even being friends with someone of a different race was considered suspicious.

Numerous laws supported apartheid. The Population Registration Act of 1950 required people to register as a certain race, giving the Department of Home Affairs a record of people by race. Pass laws required Black men over the age of 16 to carry a reference book, which included name and employment information. Pass laws were designed to limit Black presence in white areas.

The government passed the Promotion of Bantu Self-Government Act in 1959. Although Bantu is a cultural group, white South Africans historically used the term for all Black people. This act forced Black South Africans to move out of towns and cities and into segregated areas on the outskirts called townships. Many people lost their homes and had to rent new places to live, often in areas far from where they worked, forcing them to travel long distances.

In March 1960, Sharpeville residents protested the pass laws. Sharpeville was one of the townships created for Black people to reside in. Police fired into the crowd, killing 69 people and injuring many more in what was called the Sharpeville Massacre.[9] In 1961, the Indemnity Act made

Signs in Afrikaans and English reinforced apartheid, declaring that certain facilities were for the use of white people only.

it legal for the police to use violence, torture, or killing to do their job. Still other laws made it legal to arrest people without trial and prevent them from seeing their families or talking to a lawyer.

On May 31, 1961, in the midst of this turmoil, South Africa became a republic. This meant that the nation was no longer under the rule of the British monarchy. It was free to elect its own president and establish a system of self-government. Under this new government, South Africa's discriminatory policies continued.

In 1974, the Afrikaans Medium Decree was passed to limit school instruction to English and Afrikaans. In 1976, thousands of children demonstrated in the township of Soweto because they wanted to be taught in English and not Afrikaans. The students viewed Afrikaans as "the language of the oppressor."[10] The police used tear gas and dogs to control the crowd. When that didn't work, they shot into the crowd, killing two students.

As a result, tensions rose in subsequent protests. Mobs targeted government workers, and the police escalated their response. In what became known as the Soweto Uprising, police killed 700 South Africans by year's end.[11] The United Nations, an international organization that promotes human rights, denounced apartheid. Many countries stopped doing business with South Africa.

Slowly, apartheid was dismantled. In 1990, South African president F. W. de Klerk abolished apartheid and the nation began transitioning to a more democratic society. Political prisoner and Black activist Nelson Mandela was released from prison.

Over the next year, Parliament repealed numerous apartheid laws and freed many political prisoners. In 1994, the first fully democratic South African election was held, and Mandela became president when the African National Congress (ANC) political party won the election. Mandela met with political leaders from throughout the country.

THE TRUTH AND RECONCILIATION COMMISSION

The Truth and Reconciliation Commission was a government body established in 1995 to uncover the truth about human rights violations during apartheid. The commission interviewed approximately 22,000 victims and gathered information from those accused of crimes. Five volumes of its report were published on October 29, 1998, and the last two were published on March 21, 2003.[12] The commission made recommendations to prevent widespread discrimination from recurring in South Africa. Other countries have formed similar groups to investigate human rights violations.

MINI **BIO**

NELSON MANDELA

Rolihlahla Mandela was born on July 18, 1918, in Eastern Cape Province. His father was the primary counselor to the Thembu people's acting king. The Thembu people were part of the Xhosa nation. Mandela listened to the elders' stories about his people's bravery in fighting the British and Boers and wanted to fight against apartheid.

In elementary school, he was given the Christian name Nelson. As an adult, he rose through the ranks of the African National Congress (ANC). The ANC protested peacefully against apartheid, but the government shot and killed unarmed demonstrators and arrested others. Eventually, Mandela came to believe that only armed struggle would defeat apartheid. He helped form the armed resistance group Spear of the Nation. He worked in secret for this group until he was arrested in 1962. In 1963, he and seven others were sentenced to life in prison and sent to Robben Island.

As part of their efforts to end apartheid, the government released Mandela from prison on February 11, 1990. In 1994, South Africa held the nation's first democratic elections. After the ANC took the majority of the votes in the election, Mandela became president, serving from 1994 to 1999. He worked for conflict resolution throughout the world until his death in 2013.

In 1993, Nelson Mandela and F. W. de Klerk shared the Nobel Peace Prize for their efforts to bring a peaceful end to apartheid in South Africa.

The Hector Pieterson Memorial remembers the 12-year-old boy who was killed by police during the Soweto Uprising. Sam Nzima's photo of Pieterson being carried by fellow students became a symbol of the struggle against apartheid.

Despite the end of apartheid, South Africa continues to struggle with segregation and inequality. When the ANC funded the construction of nearly two million homes for Black South Africans from 1994 to 2004, the homes were built in the townships, where many areas still have no access to utilities such as running water. Residents face long commutes to reach their jobs in the cities, where many earn low pay.[13]

Furthermore, Black South Africans continue to be forced back into the townships. As urban areas are improved, food stalls and expensive stores replace the homes of the urban poor. Many of those displaced are Black people, who are forced to find cheap housing, which is often located in the townships.

CHAPTER **FIVE**

PEOPLE AND CULTURE

Approximately 60.5 million people lived in South Africa in 2024. Of these people, 81 percent are Black Africans, 9 percent are Coloured or mixed-race, 8 percent are white, and 3 percent are Indian or Asian. South Africa has 12 official languages, and most people speak at least two.[1] English is the language spoken in public, especially in the cities. English is also used when dealing with the government, in business, and in the media. But many people have another language they speak at home.

Among these is the language of the Zulu people, isiZulu. When asked about their home language, 25 percent of South Africans said they speak isiZulu at home. Only 9 percent speak English at home, and

Public markets, including Melville Food and Farmer's Market and Bryanston Market, are popular gathering spots for South Africans in Johannesburg.

Signs around South Africa may be translated into many different languages. There are 12 official languages, but there are 11 additional languages that are spoken in different parts of the country.

12 percent speak Afrikaans. Besides isiZulu, there are several widely spoken African languages. About 15 percent of people speak isiXhosa at home. This is followed by Sepedi at 10 percent, Setswana at 9 percent, Sesotho at 8 percent, Xitsonga at 4 percent, siSwati at 3 percent, Tshivenda at 3 percent, and isiNdebele at 2 percent. Another 2 percent speak other languages. These include South African sign language, which is an official language, and Khoi languages, which are not.[2]

When polled about the religions they practice, 86 percent of South Africans said they are Christian. Traditional African religions are practiced by 5 percent of the people. Some of these religions focus on ancestors, while others focus on the spirits of nonhuman things. Of the remaining people, 2 percent are Muslim, and 5 percent practice no religion.[3]

MUSIC, ART, AND MORE

South Africa has a rich and diverse music scene. South African jazz combines local and international influences, including Black American music. This jazz also draws on the music of Africa. Under apartheid, jazz was a form of protest in the townships, although it is now established throughout the country. Noteworthy musicians include Hugh Masekela and Sylvia Mdunyelwa.

Marabi emerged in the 1920s as people of color moved into urban areas. This style of music combined jazz keyboards with traditional African sounds. It was played to attract people to shebeens, which were similar to British pubs with drinks, socializing, and dancing. Shebeens were once illegal but are now popular places for people to gather.

TRADITIONAL MUSICAL INSTRUMENTS

Traditional instruments are part of South African music. One of these is the ramkie guitar, which was originally made with a gourd as the body. The modern version uses an oil can instead and includes three or four fishing wire strings. Street vendors sell oil can ramkies to tourists. The marimba is a wooden xylophone played by street performers, but it is also used as an accompaniment when choirs sing traditional songs.

Modern South African music covers a variety of sounds. The Soweto String Quartet combines classical string instruments with the guitar of another style of South African music, mbaqanga, as well as the vocals of gospel. Even after his death in 2002, Johannes Kerkorrel is still well-known for alternative Afrikaans music full of lyrics that mocked apartheid and spoke out on issues in South African life. Brasse Vannie Kaap, a group that performs rap, is also popular.

South Africa is home to international entertainers as well. Comedian and television host Trevor Noah is best known in the United States for hosting the comedy news program *The Daily Show* from 2015 to 2022. His mother was Xhosa and his father was a white man from Switzerland. Under apartheid, their relationship was illegal. Noah was born in 1984 during apartheid. Under apartheid laws, his parents were not allowed to live together. To even be seen together in public was very dangerous. However, Noah and his mother would quietly visit his father.

At the Summer Olympic Games, South Africa won a total of 95 Olympic medals through 2024, including 28 gold.[4]

The earliest South African art was San rock art, and the art form inspires the work of many artists today. Jane Alexander is the sculptor of *Butcher Boys*. Inspired by life under apartheid, it depicts three life-size figures with no mouths who are split down the back to expose their broken skeletons. Mmakgabo Mmapula Helen Sebidi creates colorful paintings depicting the everyday lives of South Africans. Willie Bester paints realistic scenes in oil and acrylic. He also creates life-size sculptures made from recycled steel, all depicting resistance.

South African literature is also known around the world. In 1991, Nadine Gordimer won the Nobel Prize for her lifetime of work, including a book of short stories about life during apartheid called *Crimes of Conscience*. Zakes Mda crafts plays, poems, and novels about life in postcolonial South Africa. His novel *The Madonna of Excelsior* was published in 2002. Critics called it one of the top ten South African books written in the Decade of Democracy, the first ten years of democratic government in South Africa.

Trevor Noah wrote *Born a Crime*, a book about his experiences growing up as a Coloured person during apartheid.

SPORTS

Sports are popular in South Africa, whether people are playing or watching, and the three most popular reflect the influence of the British. They are soccer, rugby, and cricket. In South Africa, soccer is called football. Soccer is especially popular among Black South Africans. Fans get into the game, blowing long plastic

The South Africa Springboks competed against the Australia Wallabies in the Rugby Championship on September 3, 2022.

horns called vuvuzelas, playing a variety of homemade instruments, and singing to show support. The men's national team is the Bafana Bafana, or the Boys, while the women's team is the Banyana Banyana, or the Girls.

In rugby, 15-player teams try to run or kick an oblong ball over the other team's goal line. They also score by kicking the ball through posts along each goal line. South Africa's national rugby team is the Springboks, also known as the Boks.

The sport of cricket shares some similarities with baseball. Teams of 11 players score points by hitting a ball with a flat bat and running between sets of wickets, or markers made of sticks. South Africa's men's national team and women's national team are both called the Proteas.

HOLIDAYS AND CELEBRATIONS

South Africans celebrate many holidays, including some that are celebrated around the world such as New Year's Day. In South Africa, New Year's festivities often last for two days beginning on December 31 with nighttime fireworks displays. Many celebrations are outside to take advantage of the summer weather.

Christmas Eve and Christmas Day are celebrated in South Africa much as they are in other countries. In towns and cities, people carol by candlelight on Christmas Eve and go to candlelit church services. Family celebrations include Christmas trees, stockings, and gifts. Christmas dinner may be turkey, a beef roast, or a braai, South

SOUTH AFRICA AT THE OLYMPICS

In June 1956, the South African government passed a law banning interracial sports. That same year, the Summer Olympics were held in Melbourne, Australia, and the Winter Olympics were held in Stockholm, Sweden. Many countries demanded that the International Olympic Committee (IOC) ban South Africa from the games. South Africa claimed its 1960 team would be interracial and was allowed to compete, but its team was all white. South Africa was not allowed to compete from 1964 to 1988. After 1991, as South Africa worked to dismantle apartheid, the nation was again allowed to compete.

African barbecue. One popular Christmas dessert is malva pudding, which is similar to a dense cake. Some people go camping for Christmas.

Easter celebrations are preceded by Lent, 40 days of fasting, praying, and penance as Christians acknowledge their flaws and shortcomings. On Easter, there are church services to celebrate the resurrection of Jesus Christ, and there are community Easter egg hunts. Many families have lunch together.

There are also holidays unique to South Africa. Every April 27, South Africans celebrate Freedom Day, which commemorates their country's first free elections in 1994. It is a way for the people to celebrate the end of apartheid and is one of the nation's 12 public holidays.[5] Some South Africans recognize Freedom Day by visiting Robben Island, where Nelson Mandela was imprisoned, or the city of Johannesburg's Apartheid Museum.

On December 16, South Africans observe the Day of Reconciliation, which marks the end of apartheid. South Africans are encouraged to learn about colonialism and how it led to racism and the system of apartheid. They consider how these issues are still influencing their lives today.

South Africans also celebrate music and art with festivals. One of the many music festivals is the Cape Town Minstrel Carnival, known in Afrikaans as the Kaapse Klopse. On January 2, thousands of minstrels, or street performers, parade through the city in makeup and costumes. The minstrels are organized into troupes, or *klopse*, of several hundred to a thousand participants. The minstrels dance, sing, and play instruments including traditional ghoema drums, trumpets, trombones, guitars, and banjos.

MINI **BIO**

DESMOND TUTU

Desmond Tutu was born of Xhosa and Tswana parents on October 7, 1931, in the town of Klerksdorp. He attended the Christian mission schools in which his father was headmaster. He became a schoolteacher in 1955 and later attended Saint Peter's Theological College in Johannesburg before being ordained as an Anglican priest in 1961. In 1962, he moved to London to attend King's College, where he earned a master of arts degree in 1966.

In 1975, he became the first Black South African to be appointed dean of Saint Mary's Cathedral in Johannesburg. He served as the bishop of Lesotho from 1976 until 1978. Then he became the general secretary of the South African Council of Churches.

In this position, he spoke out for the rights of Black South Africans under apartheid. He said that other countries should refuse to do business with South Africa and that the South African people should focus on nonviolent protest. With the end of apartheid, Tutu encouraged South Africans to think of their country as a Rainbow Nation of many peoples. He was supportive of Nelson Mandela and was made the head of the Truth and Reconciliation Commission. Tutu died on December 26, 2021, in Cape Town.

For advocating against apartheid, Desmond Tutu was awarded the Nobel Peace Prize in 1984 and the Presidential Medal of Freedom in 2009.

Minstrels in Cape Town celebrate the Second New Year, a festival known as the Cape Town Minstrel Carnival, on January 2.

The Cape Town International Jazz Festival takes place the last weekend of March at the Cape Town International Convention Centre. Thousands of people come to hear their favorite artists perform live. Performers range from new talent to big-name performers, such as Lauryn Hill and Earth, Wind & Fire.

FOOD

South African foods are a combination of many cuisines, but Dutch and Asian foods are prominent. Many South Africans say their national dish is bobotie. In this baked dish, ground lamb or beef is blended with turmeric, cumin, and curry powder. The beef is combined with bread soaked in milk, onions, and raisins. A blend of egg and milk is poured over the top. Bobotie is served with yellow rice, which is rice seasoned with turmeric, a ground root that turns the rice yellow.

Another popular dish is *potjiekos*, which means "small pot food." This stew of meat and vegetables is traditionally cooked over an open fire in a cast-iron pot or *potjie*. The ingredients are layered in the pot, and the stew is not stirred during cooking.

Pap or mealie pap is a cornmeal-based dish that is eaten as a breakfast porridge and as a braai side dish. At a braai, it can be cooked until stiff and then eaten with the fingers and used to scoop up a variety of sauces and sides including *chakalaka*, a vegetable dish of beans, onions, peppers, carrots, and spices. Another popular side is *braaied mielies*, or corn on the cob.

BUNNY CHOW

The names of some South African foods can be misleading to Americans. Bunny chow, also called Durban bunny chow or bunny, is an Indian-inspired dish popular in Durban, South Africa. Despite the name, it doesn't involve rabbit. Instead, it is made with lamb curry scooped into a hollowed loaf of bread. Modern vegetarian versions are made with bean or lentil curry. Bunny chow is believed to have been created by Indian immigrants for an easy, no-utensils lunch on the job.

CHAPTER **SIX**

POLITICS

The Republic of South Africa is a parliamentary republic, consisting of three government branches, the legislative, executive, and judicial. The people of South Africa vote for members of the legislative branch, which includes Parliament. These members of Parliament vote on legislation. The executive branch consists of the cabinet and the president, who enforce the law of the land. The judicial branch is the nation's court system. It interprets and applies the laws.

Unlike many other countries with multibranch governments, South Africa has not one capital but three, one for each branch of government. The president and cabinet form the executive branch, which is in Pretoria. South Africa's legislative branch is in Cape Town.

The Union Buildings in Pretoria are home to the offices of the president and cabinet.

The judicial branch, including the Supreme Court of Appeal, is in Bloemfontein.

In March 2024, South Africa's cabinet had 32 ministers and 43 deputy ministers.[2]

EXECUTIVE BRANCH

The president is the head of South Africa's executive branch. The president is elected not by voters but by the National Assembly, one of the houses of Parliament. The president serves up to two five-year terms. The president develops national policy and can suggest changes to existing legislation.

The cabinet is also part of the executive branch and is made of ministers appointed by the president. Ministers are chosen from the National Assembly, and their number varies from cabinet to cabinet. Each cabinet minister is given one or more areas of responsibility, known as portfolios. The 27 South African portfolios include subjects such as health, police, and transportation.[1] Each minister has one or two deputies and a small team of advisers to assist in their work.

PARLIAMENT

The legislative branch of South Africa's federal government is called Parliament. Parliament includes two houses, the National Assembly and the National Council of Provinces (NCOP). The two houses select their membership in different ways.

The National Assembly is selected through proportional representation elections. This means that voters cast ballots for political parties, not individual candidates. Before the election, each political party submits a numbered list of candidates in order of preference. Everyone over the age of 18 is eligible to vote for the political parties, and the numbers are totaled. There are 400 parliamentary seats, and each party gets an allocation based on how many votes they won in the election. A party that won 10 percent of the votes gets 10 percent of the seats, or 40 seats. The first 40 people on the party's numbered list become members of parliament (MPs).

The first order of business for the National Assembly is to choose the president. Then it passes laws and watches over the executive branch to make certain this branch performs its duties as required. The National Assembly is where representatives of the South African people publicly debate vital issues, such as how to reduce poverty and crime, provide clean water and housing to all citizens, or improve transportation and other forms of infrastructure.

The National Council of Provinces includes 90 provincial delegates, with ten delegates from each province. Of these ten, six are permanent delegates and four are special delegates. Permanent delegates are chosen by the provincial legislatures. The four special delegates include

THE SEVENTH SOUTH AFRICAN PARLIAMENT

Every five years, the people of South Africa cast their votes for Parliament's National Assembly. Each Parliament is named with a number, beginning with the First Parliament, which convened in 1910 after the country became independent from Britain. The parliament that convened in 1994 after the first democratic election was the Twenty-Second Parliament. But the South African government considered it the First Parliament, resetting the count to coincide with the beginning of democratic elections. The Seventh Parliament convened in 2024.

the premier of the province and three special delegates from the provincial legislature. The special delegates rotate depending on what topic is currently in front of the NCOP.

The NCOP makes sure that concerns brought forward from the provinces are considered in the national government. The NCOP evaluates and votes on legislation. It also provides a forum for concerns to be heard.

THE JUDICIAL BRANCH

The judicial branch is known as the judiciary. The lowest courts are called Magistrates' Courts, and they hear cases involving evictions, divorce, child custody, and domestic violence as well as civil cases such as lawsuits. South Africa is divided into 354 magisterial districts, each with its own court. More serious crimes such as murder, rape, and armed robbery are dealt with in Regional Magistrates' Courts.

The High Court is two levels above Magistrates' Courts. The president of South Africa appoints High Court judges. The High Court has seats, or locations, throughout South Africa. This court hears appeals from the lower courts as well as any cases that happen outside the scope or jurisdiction

PROVINCES AND LOCAL GOVERNMENTS

Each province has its own legislature. These legislatures have one house, instead of the two in the national Parliament, and range from 30 to 80 members who are elected for five-year terms. Each legislature elects a premier, who appoints a provincial executive council of up to ten people. South Africa is also divided into 257 municipalities, some of which have mayors and some of which have councils. Municipal governments of all types are tasked with growing local economies and maintaining infrastructure such as roads, water, sanitation, and lighting in public areas.

Legislators meet to present, discuss, and pass laws in the Houses of Parliament building in Cape Town, South Africa.

The Supreme Court of Appeal is located in Bloemfontein, Free State, South Africa. In September 2024, Mandisa Muriel Lindelwa Maya became the first female chief justice of the Republic of South Africa.

of the lower courts, such as treason. People who believe they were wrongly convicted or fined can file an appeal and the High Court may decide to review the case. These cases are reviewed by two judges.

The Supreme Court of Appeal in Bloemfontein is a level above the High Courts. A judge president presides over the Supreme Court, which rules on all appeals except those relating to the constitution. The Constitutional Court in Johannesburg hears all cases relating to the constitution. It is also the final court of appeals and is presided over by the chief justice of South Africa.

POLITICAL PARTIES

From the end of apartheid in 1990 until 2024, the ANC held a majority of the parliamentary seats. But the ANC lost this majority in 2024. Critics believe this was because voters were frustrated by issues such as high crime rates and unreliable electric service. Although it no longer had a majority in the National Assembly, the ANC was one of ten parties that agreed to work together in a new Unity Government formed in 2024.[3]

The members of the Unity Government represent a wide range of South Africa's political interests and parties. The ANC held 159 Parliamentary seats. With 17 seats, the Inkatha Freedom Party is a conservative party with strong support among the Zulu people. The Pan Africanist Congress of Azania, which believes that people of African descent should unite, had one seat.[4]

Other parties that secured seats strongly represent white South Africans. The Democratic Alliance is a white-majority, pro-business party. It earned 87 seats in 2024. The Patriotic Alliance, a new party with nine seats, has a strong anti-immigration stance. With six seats, Freedom Front Plus is a white conservative party popular among Afrikaans speakers that traditionally works to minimize the power of the ANC.[5]

Many new political parties earned seats in 2024. uMkhonto weSizwe, a Zulu nationalist party, ran on an anti-foreigner platform and earned 58 seats. The Economic Freedom Fighters, which present themselves as anti-capitalists, won 39 seats. ActionSA is a party based on social justice. It won 6 seats. Other new parties included Rise Mzansi, Build One SA, Cape Coloured Congress, and United Africans Transformation, which each secured one or two seats.[6]

SOUTH AFRICAN NATIONAL DEFENSE FORCE

The South African military is known as the South African National Defense Force (SANDF). The SANDF defends the territory of South Africa on land and at sea. It consists of 40,000 members

The SANDF takes part in international African and UN peacekeeping missions.

of the South African Army, 7,000 members of the South African Navy, 10,000 members of the South African Air Force, and 8,000 members of the South African Military Health Service.[7] The Military Health Service provides health care to soldiers, veterans, and their dependents.

In 1994, the SANDF replaced the South African Defense Force, which was composed almost entirely of white South Africans. The SANDF is open to all South African citizens who are 18 to 22 years old, have completed grade 12, and have no criminal record. Members of the SANDF serve for two years. In 2023, women made up nearly 30 percent of the military.[8]

SYMBOLS OF SOUTH AFRICA

Meant to be temporary, the South African flag was designed by state herald Frederick Brownell. The state herald works within the

National Archives, a national library that preserves documents and items related to South Africa's identity. Brownell was asked to design a new flag in February 1994. He was given one week to come up with a flag that symbolized unity.

The flag he created features a Y shape, symbolizing two paths coming together for a common future. The colorful flag includes yellow, white, red, black, green, and blue. These colors are meaningful to different groups of South African people.

South Africa's national anthem, "Nkosi Sikelel' iAfrika," combines "God Bless Africa" ("Nkosi Sikelel' iAfrika") and "The Call of South Africa" ("Die Stem van Suid-Afrika"). "Nkosi Sikelel' iAfrika" was a popular Xhosa language church hymn sung at political rallies. "The Call of South Africa" was a poem later set to music that became the first national anthem in 1959. The anthem has verses in Xhosa, Zulu, Sesotho, and Afrikaans. It ends with a powerful message. "Sounds the call to come together / And united we shall stand / Let us live and strive for freedom / In South Africa our land."[9]

BUREAU OF HERALDRY

The Bureau of Heraldry is part of the national government. The constitution states that anyone can register a coat of arms, which is a decorative shield that represents the person's family. It also registers and keeps track of city flags, uniforms, badges, and other symbols of authority for the nation as a whole, the provinces, and the various South African cities. One requirement of a new coat of arms is that it not resemble too closely another coat of arms that has already been registered.

CHAPTER **SEVEN**

ECONOMICS

A nation's economy is a measure of wealth and resources within that country. The value of the goods and services produced by a country over a set period of time is its gross domestic product (GDP). In 2024, South Africa had an estimated GDP of nearly $400 billion.[1]

South Africa has the largest economy in Africa in large part because of the nation's mineral wealth. South Africa is one of the world's biggest producers of gold. The nation has abundant gold reserves remaining. In 2022, South Africa exported $22.7 billion in gold, making it the fifth-largest exporter of this mineral worldwide.[2] Gold from South Africa is exported to China, Switzerland, India, the United Arab Emirates, and Hong Kong. Through 2006, South Africa had been the world's largest exporter of gold, but investment

Gold was discovered in the Johannesburg area in 1886. By 1899, the South African gold mining industry supplied nearly a third of the world's gold and provided jobs for more than 100,000 people.

in South African gold mining has dropped. This is due to an unreliable supply of electricity, illegal mining, and theft. As a result, profits have also dropped.

Another valuable South African mineral is coal. South African coal is used to generate electricity within the country as well as for export. In 2023, South Africa exported $9.8 billion worth of coal, mostly to India, South Korea, Italy, and Japan.[3]

South Africa is also the world's largest exporter of platinum and chromium. In 2023, it exported $16.2 billion in platinum, mainly to the United States, the United Kingdom, and China. That same year, the country exported $6.3 billion in chromium ore, mainly to China and Mozambique.[4] Platinum is a precious metal used in jewelry and electrical devices. Chromium is used to manufacture steel, cast iron, and pigments. It is also used in metal plating and to tan leather.

Another critical export for South Africa is diamonds. In 2023, South Africa exported $6.4 billion in diamonds to China, the United Arab Emirates, Belgium, and the United States.[5] Not all of these diamonds were mounted or set into jewelry.

THE HISTORY OF DIAMOND MINING

In 1867, diamonds were found along the Orange, Vaal, and Harts Rivers. By the end of 1871, nearly 50,000 people lived in the center of this area in a mining camp called Kimberley.[6] Initially, Black and white miners labored side by side, but this changed as mining transitioned from digging by hand to mechanical digging. In 1889, De Beers Consolidated Mines, under the direction of mining operator Cecil Rhodes, took over all the diamond mining. Some whites continued to work as overseers, but most workers were Black African immigrants who, when not working, were confined to closed compounds.

Instead, they were industrial diamonds. These stones, which are flawed, oddly shaped, or unattractive in color, are used in metalworking and mining to cut or polish other things.

Many other minerals are mined in South Africa. Iron ore is used to make iron and various types of steel. Manganese is also used in manufacturing iron. Copper is an excellent conductor, so it is used to manufacture electrical wiring and motors. Titanium, which can resist high temperatures and is also lightweight, is used in the aerospace industry. Beryllium is a lightweight metal used in spacecraft as well as in nuclear reactors.

Manufacturing employs more of South Africa's people and contributes more to the GDP than mining. Yet mining is still at the center of the nation's economy. This is because companies that invest in mining also invest in other areas of the economy.

South Africa exported about 57.8 million short tons (52.4 million metric tons) of iron ore in 2023.

INDUSTRY

Although only about one-tenth of South Africa's surface area has sufficiently good soil and water resources to grow crops, agriculture is a vital industry.[7] Through irrigation, some dry areas have been farmed to grow a variety of crops. Major crops include corn, wheat, sugarcane, sorghum, peanuts, tobacco, and various fruits, including citrus.

Sheep, goats, cattle, and pigs are raised for food and also for other products, such as wool. Dairy products, including butter, cheese, and eggs, are produced near major cities. Fishing is another important industry. In the waters off the western and southern coasts, fishers bring in sole; maasbanker, or mackerel; kingklip, which is an eel; and hake.

Agricultural products and fish are then processed. Sugarcane is refined into sugar, and fruits are canned. More than half of South Africa's food products are exported to other countries.

Chemical production and manufacturing also form an important part of the economy. This industry began by producing explosives for mining. Coal is used to make plastics, resins, and other industrial chemicals. South Africa also manufactures automobiles, ships, building materials, electronics, and weapons.

Another critical South African industry is tourism. In 2023, nearly 8.5 million international visitors traveled to South Africa. This is more than had visited the country the preceding year as tourism rebounded after the early COVID-19 pandemic.[8] They come to bask on its beaches and photograph its scenery and wildlife. They also come to visit United Nations Educational, Scientific and Cultural Organization (UNESCO) sites. These are places around the world that UNESCO has

South Africa is a major producer of citrus, growing mandarins, lemons, oranges, and grapefruit.

The Blyde River Canyon near Kruger National Park is a popular stop with tourists.

declared of cultural or natural importance to humankind. Among South Africa's 12 UNESCO World Heritage sites are locations where early human fossils were found, Robben Island, and Maloti-Drakensberg Park, which contains 690 examples of prehistoric rock art.[9]

ANTI-APARTHEID BOYCOTTS AND SANCTIONS

Starting in the 1960s, apartheid isolated not only Black South Africans but the entire nation. In 1968, South Africa refused to let England's cricket team enter the country because player Basil D'Oliveira was mixed-race. This led to South Africa being banned from international competitions in cricket, rugby, and other sports. People around the world objected to apartheid policies, and slowly, foreign businesses and governments listened. By 1985, foreign banks called in South Africa's loans, which meant they had to be paid in full. American churches, universities, and other organizations demanded the US government and companies stop doing business with South Africa. Global economic pressure played a part in bringing apartheid to an end.

TRANSPORTATION AND TELEPHONES

South Africa has a varied transportation system. The railway system serves major cities, most smaller towns, and many rural areas. It is largely owned and operated as part of the government-owned transportation system, Passenger Rail Agency of South Africa (PRASA). There are 19,000 miles (31,000 km) of track, and more than 80 percent of the system is electric.[10] Although few people use trains to travel long distances, commuter trains are popular in the cities.

In addition to railroads, there are 185,000 miles (298,000 km) of roads in South Africa. These include multilane freeways and unpaved rural roads. About 40 percent of the roads are paved.[11]

Two-lane highways run between most towns, and four-lane roads are almost entirely limited to the major cities.

A lot of South Africans get from place to place on these roads. But in 2021, only 37 percent of all South African households owned a car.[12] About 69 percent of South African households rely on minibus taxis, which are small passenger vans.[13] This industry is unregulated because vans are privately owned and not registered with the government. Many owners and drivers are Black, and the industry was born during apartheid when Black South Africans needed to get from their homes in the townships to their jobs.

Air service makes it possible to travel across the vast nation quickly. The state-owned South African Airways and several private competitors provide freight and passenger air travel. All these carriers fly between South Africa and its neighboring countries. The central airport for both domestic and international flights is O. R. Tambo International Airport near Johannesburg. There are also major airports with international flights in Cape Town and Durban.

In December 2024, 1,000 rand was worth $54.37 in US dollars.[15]

Another government-owned service is Telkom, South Africa's telecommunications company. Since 1991 it has been 70 percent government owned and 30 percent owned by private investors.[14] Telecommunication services in South Africa are well developed where they exist, but availability is uneven. However, more people are gaining access. By March 2024, 20.4 million users had cell phone service through Telkom, making it the third-largest provider in South Africa after the private companies Vodacom, with 59.9 million users, and MTN, with 37.7 million users.[16]

BEFORE THE RAND

When the Cape Colony was first founded, people paid for items with gold mohurs and rupees, both from India, doubloons from the Spanish empire, and English shillings. In 1806, when the British took over, the prevailing currency was paper rix-dollars, first printed and issued by Dutch authorities in 1782. The British intended to replace the rix-dollar with printed pounds, but they printed additional rix-dollars as well. In 1910, the British pound was used as currency in South Africa. The rand replaced the pound in 1961.

MONEY

The South African currency is the rand, and each rand is divided into 100 cents. *Rand* is abbreviated as *R*. Coins are available in denominations of five cents, ten cents, 20 cents, and 50 cents. If an item costs 50 rand and 40 cents, it is written R50,40. The coins include images of South African plants and animals.

Rand banknotes are adorned with images of South African wildlife. A rhinoceros appears on the ten-rand note, an elephant is on the 20-rand note, a lion is on the 50-rand note, a buffalo appears on the 100-rand note, and a leopard is on the 200-rand note. All South African money is issued by the South African Reserve Bank.

South Africans used British pound sterling until 1921, when the South African pound was introduced. In 1961, South Africa became a republic and rolled out the rand. This is short for *Witwatersrand*, which translates to "ridge of white waters." Witwatersrand is a rocky area where most of South Africa's gold deposits were found.

An image of Nelson Mandela first appeared on the front of South Africa's rand notes in 2012.

ECONOMIC DIFFICULTIES

One of the greatest economic challenges that South Africa faces is inequality. Between 2005 and 2010, the percentage of the population living below the poverty line dropped from 68 percent to 56 percent, but by 2023 it had increased to 62 percent.[17] The World Bank, an international banking organization, defines the poverty line as the least amount of money someone can make to purchase what they need to live.

There are many reasons that South Africans are having trouble increasing their incomes. One problem is the high unemployment rate, which reached 33.5 percent in the second quarter of 2024, the period from April through June. This rate is higher than unemployment was before the early COVID-19 pandemic.[18]

A strong economy relies on transporting goods to market efficiently. The state-owned freight transit system, Transnet, has deteriorated because of poor management, theft, vandalism, and sabotage. Many of its locomotives are several decades old, which means they often need repair and are unreliable. The shortage of trains has led major industries, such as mining, to rely on trucks to transport goods to ports. Traffic congestion at major ports, such as Durban, delays the import and export of goods by several weeks.

Due to these issues and failure of the aging equipment used to load ships, ports operated by Transnet are inefficient. The ports at Cape Town and Ngqura are ranked as the two worst in the world by the World Bank.[19] Because of poor performance, Transnet's South African ports lose business to more efficient African ports, such as Berbera and Mogadishu in Somalia and Conakry in Guinea.

CHAPTER **EIGHT**

SOUTH AFRICA TODAY

In South Africa today, people find a variety of ways to entertain themselves. Some ways date back to apartheid, when it was illegal for Black people to meet in groups of more than three people and public dancing was against the law. Despite these laws, as Black South Africans found work in the cities, they needed places they could go to have fun, and the answer was the shebeen.

Shebeens are like local taverns with food and drink where neighbors gather. Shebeen queens were the women who brewed their own beer and sold it in their shebeens. Shebeens are still popular in townships,

Hundreds of beaches line South Africa's coast. The most popular are located around Durban, on the Cape Peninsula, and along the Garden Route in the Western Cape.

and people meet to have a drink and order traditional food such as *umfino*, a stew made with spinach-like greens, and pap served with chakalaka.

Families in South Africa often spend time at the park or the beach. People may go to the beach for watersports such as surfing, windsurfing, or swimming. Other beaches are great places to see wildlife or go horseback riding.

People also enjoy South Africa's many festivals and events. The Hermanus Whale Festival celebrates the return of southern right whales to Walker Bay. It takes place in September every year and is one of the few places where people can watch whales from land. The annual sardine run is another opportunity to enjoy nature. Every year, enormous groups, or shoals, of sardines return to the KwaZulu-Natal coast, attracting birds and sharks as well as fishers. People come to see bottlenose dolphins, copper sharks, whales, and seabirds, such as cormorants and gulls, feast on sardines. The Iconic Bastille Festival, a celebration of French culture, takes place in July on the Franschhoek High School grounds.

Cape Town has 72 public beaches.[1]

Open-air markets are popular throughout South Africa. People visit them with their friends and families. Greenmarket Square is the oldest market in Cape Town, and vendors arrive every morning to share their wares with passersby. Visitors stroll the cobbled streets, browsing various stalls selling food, clothing, jewelry, leather goods such as sandals, and even paintings. Bargaining is a big part of the market experience, as visitors strive for a good price.

Southern right whales come to the shallow waters off the coast of Hermanus, Western Cape, South Africa, in June and stay through November to mate.

EDUCATION

Throughout the year, young people in South Africa attend public or private schools. Public schools are funded by the government. Students complete four terms that run through the entire year.

The quality of public school education varies greatly, with many rural schools and schools in impoverished areas lacking basics such as clean water and electricity. Not all students have access to learning materials, and teacher quality and training are not consistent. Because of these challenges, many students fail basic literacy and mathematics tests. To solve some of these problems, a movement is underway to expand the use of technology in the classroom, but many rural schools lack internet access.

Private schools in South Africa are similar to those in the United States. They are privately owned, and students must pay tuition fees to attend them. Many parents who can afford to do so send their children to private schools, which offer smaller class sizes and better facilities. Only about 5 percent of children attend these schools because of the high costs to go there.[2] The most expensive private school in the country is Hilton College in

BANTU EDUCATION ACT

The Bantu Education Act went into effect in 1954, creating government schools under the Department of Native Affairs. Black children had to attend these schools and were taught in their own languages as well as having classes in English and Afrikaans. Students studied math, social studies, and the Christian religion. They also studied planting, soil conservation, and handicrafts including needlework. These schools were underfunded, with class sizes of between 40 and 60 students per instructor.[3] The curriculum focused on what Black students needed to know to work for white South Africans.

KwaZulu-Natal, where students must live on campus. Annual fees for tuition, room, and board in late 2024 were R397 660 ($21,974.85).[4]

All students begin with a required year of pre-primary education called Reception Year or Grade R when they are five to six years old. They learn to think critically, solve problems, interact with other children, communicate, and work with others. Students then go on to primary school, which is grades 1 to 7 for ages six to 12 years. In grades 1 through 3, students learn to read and do math. In grades 4 through 6, they add social studies and science.

Secondary school is grades 8 through 12 for ages 13 to 18 years. This is often called high school, and students can legally quit school after completing grade 9. In grades 7 through 9, students study mathematics, science, technology, economics, arts and culture, and two of South Africa's official languages.

When students start grade 10, they choose to study a vocational stream of education or an academic stream of education. The vocational

WILDLIFE MANAGEMENT INTERNSHIP

Global Vision International (GVI) offers a six-month wildlife management internship at a game reserve in Limpopo. It involves collecting data about predators such as lions, leopards, and cheetahs and large herbivores, including rhinos and elephants, because these are the animals that have the most influence in a small reserve. But GVI interns also work in the local community. They may teach at the village primary school or help with building projects in the village itself, with the goal of showing students the kind of effect their actions can have on the world.

Overcrowding is a major problem in many rural schools in South Africa. There are not enough teachers or classrooms to accommodate the number of students, who are sometimes forced to share desks.

stream is similar to vocational colleges in the United States. Students in this stream learn whatever skills are needed to enter a specific career in the trades, such as an electrician or welder. The academic stream leads to a four-year college or university.

All students in grades 10 through 12 take two official languages, mathematics, and life orientation. This required class helps students develop self-awareness, social skills, and decision-making skills. Other classes are based on their interests and whether they have chosen an academic stream or a vocational stream. Some may study arts, science, technology, business courses, agriculture, and career-oriented courses.

From October to December, students in their final year of high school can elect to take the National State Curriculum exam. This exam tests them in two South African languages, mathematics, life orientation, and

The University of the Witwatersrand in Johannesburg is one of 26 public universities in South Africa.

three elective subjects. Depending on their score, students can attend university or a Technical Vocational Education and Training (TVET) college.

University students study for three to six years. They can also take part in internships, learning on the job. University students may earn a variety of degrees similar to those offered at schools in the United States.

South Africans who want to pursue a technical vocation may attend a TVET college. Found across the country, these schools offer hands-on training in various areas such as engineering, business, and hospitality, which includes hotel management. TVET colleges are less expensive than universities and make higher-level education accessible to more people.

Learnerships are another way to learn job skills in South Africa. They combine classroom learning and on-the-job training. Learnerships are available in fields such as welding, boilermaking, and engineering.

Someone who wants to work in a technical field may also look for an apprenticeship. An apprenticeship gives an inexperienced worker the opportunity to learn as they work alongside one or more experienced professionals. Apprenticeships are available for positions in a wide range of fields, including those of mechanics and electricians.

MODERN PROBLEMS

The World Inequality Lab studies economic disparities around the globe. In 2021, it found that the richest 10 percent of the population in South Africa controlled 85 percent of the wealth.[5]

SOUTH AFRICA AND CLIMATE CHANGE

Because South Africa depends on coal to generate electricity, it is one of the world's top 15 greenhouse gas emitters. Burning coal releases carbon dioxide, a greenhouse gas, into the atmosphere. This gas traps heat instead of allowing it to radiate into space, and this trapped heat increases average temperatures. Since 1990, South Africa's national average temperature has increased twice as fast as global temperatures. Because of these temperature increases, South Africa will likely become hotter and drier. This change in climate will alter agriculture and lead to extreme weather including droughts.[11]

The group described South Africa as having the highest income inequality in the world. In 2023, approximately 13 million people lived in poverty with less than US $2.15 to meet their daily needs for food, clothing, and housing.[6]

One reason for this poverty is the unemployment rate. In 2024, the unemployment rate in South Africa hovered between 32 and 34 percent.[7] The rate is especially high for young people 15 to 24 years old at 60.8 percent.[8]

Poverty aggravates other problems. By 2022, 89.6 percent of all households had electricity, but Eskom, the national electrical utility, cannot generate enough electricity to meet demand.[9] To keep from overloading their equipment, Eskom uses a planned series of rolling blackouts, which may mean an area has no electricity for up to 12 hours a day.[10] Some people buy generators, allowing them to produce their own electricity for pumping water, preparing food, and accessing the internet for school and work. But people living below the poverty line cannot afford to buy generators.

Access to running water is also a problem in South Africa. By 2023, 80.4 percent of all households were connected to government-provided water. But major discrepancies remained

Residents of Diepsloot, a township north of Johannesburg, gather water at a local water source. The town was originally a temporary camp for refugees, but many stayed permanently and in 2025, more than 350,000 people still lived there.

between wealthy and poor areas. In 2022, 85.5 percent of homes in Western Cape had access to tap water, while only 31.4 percent of homes in Limpopo, the poorest province, had access.[12]

Experts note that poverty and unemployment drive crime, which was at an all-time high in South Africa in the early 2020s. From 2022 to 2023, kidnappings increased by 41.7 percent and carjackings increased by 8.5 percent.[13] People are kidnapped and forced to turn over their cell phones and passwords so that thieves can empty their bank accounts. This crime rate has led to an increase in the number of private security guards hired by those who can afford them. Between 2013 and 2023 there was a 44 percent jump in the number of registered security guards. In 2023, there were 2.7 million security guards compared with fewer than 150,000 police officers.[14]

The US State Department advises American citizens to use extreme caution when visiting South Africa. American travelers have been targeted for kidnapping and robbery. Travelers are advised not to travel alone and to use only well-maintained highways. They should avoid the townships unless they are with a local guide.

South Africa continues to face the challenges created by apartheid as the nation works to provide equal access to learning and resources for all South Africans. This includes building and maintaining infrastructure that provides people with basic necessities such as clean water, electricity, and reliable transportation. It also includes trying to balance South Africa's extreme income inequality. Despite these challenges, South Africa is a country with a lot to offer both the people who live there and those who visit. A wide variety of cultures have created music and art like no others in the world, and the landscapes and wildlife are unparalleled.

ESSENTIAL **FACTS**

OFFICIAL NAME: REPUBLIC OF SOUTH AFRICA

GEOGRAPHY

Area: 470,693 square miles (1,219,090 sq km)

Highest Elevation: Mafadi Peak (Ntheledi) at 11,320 feet (3,450 m)

Lowest Elevation: Atlantic Ocean at 0 feet (0 m)

PEOPLE

Population: 60.4 million (2024 est.)

Most Populous City: Cape Town (3.4 million)

Ethnic Groups: Black African, Coloured, white, Indian/Asian

Religions: Christianity; ancestral, tribal, animist or other traditional African religions; Islam; other; none

GOVERNMENT

Type of Government: Parliamentary republic

Capital: Pretoria, Cape Town, and Bloemfontein

Head of State and Government: President

Legislature: Bicameral, with a National Council of Provinces and a National Assembly

ECONOMY

Currency: Rand

Major Industries: Mining, agriculture and foodstuffs, metalworking, machinery, chemicals

Natural Resources: Gold, coal, platinum, chromium, diamonds, iron ore, copper

NATIONAL SYMBOLS

National Anthem: "Nkosi Sikelel' iAfrika"

National Animal: Springbok

National Flower: King protea

GLOSSARY

abolish
To put an end to or cancel.

aerospace
Related to the manufacturing industry that specializes in aircraft and spacecraft.

colonize
To send a group of settlers to an area and assume political control of the area.

democratic
Based on a form of government in which people choose leaders by voting.

drainage basin
An area of land from which all water runs into a single river or lake.

headwaters
The source of a river.

jurisdiction
A certain area within which a group has authority to make a legal decision or take legal action.

migrate
To move from habitat to habitat based on the seasons.

navigable
Deep enough and with no obstacles so that ships can sail through.

nectar
A sugary liquid produced by flowering plants to attract pollinators.

pastoralist
A person who raises herd animals such as sheep or cattle.

penance
An act that makes up for wrongdoing or sinning.

terrace
One of a series of flat areas that form massive steps down a slope.

veteran
A person who served in the military.

vocational
Related to a skill or trade that can be pursued as a career.

ADDITIONAL **RESOURCES**

SELECTED BIBLIOGRAPHY

"Amazing Adaptations: South African Ostrich." *Kariega Game Reserve*, n.d., kariega.co.za. Accessed 27 Nov. 2024.

"The Arrival of the Khoisan." *South African History Online*, 16 Jan. 2020, sahistory.org.za. Accessed 27 Nov. 2024.

"Climate Risk Country Profile: South Africa." *World Bank Group*, 2021, climageknowledgeportal.worldbank.org. Accessed 6 Dec. 2024.

FURTHER READINGS

Conyngham, Richard. *All Rise: Resistance and Rebellion in South Africa*. Catalyst, 2021.

DK South Africa. DK, 2023.

Kolisi, Siya. *Rise*. HarperCollins, 2021.

ONLINE RESOURCES

To learn more about South Africa, please visit **abdobooklinks.com** or scan this QR code. These links are routinely monitored and updated to provide the most current information available.

MORE INFORMATION

For more information on this subject, contact or visit the following organizations:

Apartheid Museum
Northern Pkwy. and Gold Reef Rd.
Ormonde, 2001
Johannesburg, South Africa
apartheidmuseum.org
Visitors to the Apartheid Museum explore what life was like under apartheid. They also learn about the various activists who helped dismantle the system.

Embassy of the Republic of South Africa
3051 Massachusetts Ave. NW
Washington, DC 20008
saembassy.org
The embassy not only represents South Africa to the United States but also educates people about the country.

The Mandela House
8115 Vilakazi St.
Orlando West, 1804
Johannesburg, South Africa
mandelahouse.com/about
Nelson Mandela's Soweto home is now a museum where visitors can learn about Mandela, historic Soweto, and apartheid.

SOURCE **NOTES**

CHAPTER 1. A TOUR OF SOUTH AFRICA

1. "A Guide to the Traditional Food of South Africa." *Scott Dunn*, 4 Jan. 2023, scottdunn.com. Accessed 4 Feb. 2025.
2. "History of the Park." *Kruger Safari Company*, n.d., krugerpark.travel. Accessed 4 Feb. 2025.
3. "Distance from Cape Town to Johannesburg." *Distance Calculator*, n.d., distance.to. Accessed 4 Feb. 2025.
4. "Table Mountain, Cape Town!" *Visit Table Mountain*, n.d. visittablemountain.com. Accessed 4 Feb. 2025.

CHAPTER 2. GEOGRAPHY

1. "South Africa Map and Satellite Image." *Geology.com*, 2025, geology.com. Accessed 4 Feb. 2025.
2. "Geography and Climate." *South African Government*, 2025, gov.za. Accessed 4 Feb. 2025.
3. "Geography and Climate."
4. Martin Hall and Randolph Vigne. "South Africa." *Britannica*, 3 Feb. 2025, britannica.com. Accessed 4 Feb. 2025.
5. Johann Cooks and George H. T. Kimble. "Veld." *Britannica*, 2025, britannica.com. Accessed 4 Feb. 2025.
6. "Witwatersrand." *Britannica*, 2025, britannica.com. Accessed 4 Feb. 2025.
7. "Geography and Climate."
8. "Kalahari." *Northern Cape*, n.d., northern-cape-info.co.za. Accessed 4 Feb. 2025.
9. "Geography and Climate."
10. Rédaction Africanews and Wandiswa Ntengento. "South Africa Battles with Water Crisis." *Africa News*, 13 Aug. 2022, africanews.com. Accessed 4 Feb. 2025.
11. "Drakensberg." *Britannica*, 19 Apr. 2024, britannica.com. Accessed 4 Feb. 2025.
12. "Drakensberg."
13. "Drakensberg."
14. "Tallest Mountains in South Africa." *WorldAtlas*, n.d., worldatlas.com. Accessed 4 Feb. 2025.
15. "Geography of South Africa." *World Fact Index*, n.d., worldfacts.us. Accessed 4 Feb. 2025.
16. "Geography of South Africa."
17. "Interesting Facts about Lesotho." *WorldAtlas*, n.d., worldatlas.com. Accessed 4 Feb. 2025.
18. "Prince Edward Island." *Britannica*, 19 Dec. 2024, britannica.com. Accessed 4 Feb. 2025.
19. David Frank Gordon and Leonard Monteath Thompson. "Relief of South Africa." *Britannica*, 3 Feb. 2025, britannica.com. Accessed 4 Feb. 2025.
20. "The Breede River—Everything You Need to Know." *Cape Tourism*, 3 Oct. 2024, capetourism.com. Accessed 4 Feb. 2025.
21. "Limpopo River." *Britannica*, n.d., britannica.com. Accessed 4 Feb. 2025.

CHAPTER 3. PLANTS AND ANIMALS

1. "Elephant." *Siyabona Africa*, 2024, krugerpark.co.za. Accessed 4 Feb. 2025.
2. "Big Five Wildlife in Kruger National Park." *Siyabona Africa*, 2024, krugerpark.co.za. Accessed 4 Feb. 2025.
3. "Big Five Wildlife in Kruger National Park."
4. "African Rhinoceros." *Siyabona Africa*, 2024, krugerpark.co.za. Accessed 4 Feb. 2025.
5. "African Buffalo." *Siyabona Africa*, 2024, krugerpark.co.za. Accessed 4 Feb. 2025.
6. "Amazing Adaptations: The South African Ostrich." *Kariega Game Reserve*, n.d., kariega.co.za. Accessed 4 Feb. 2025.
7. Sarah McPherson. "Just How Are Cheetahs Able to Run So Fast?" *Discover Wildlife*, 18 Dec. 2024, discoverwildlife.com. Accessed 4 Feb. 2025.
8. "Commonly Highly Dangerous Snakes of South Africa." *Siyabona Africa*, 2024, krugerpark.co.za. Accessed 4 Feb. 2025.
9. "Africa Tortoise Guide." *Siyabona Africa*, 2024, krugerpark.co.za. Accessed 4 Feb. 2025.
10. "Hippo." *Siyabona Africa*, 2024, krugerpark.co.za. Accessed 4 Feb. 2025.
11. "Crocodile." *South Africa Venues*, 2025, sa-venues.com. Accessed 4 Feb. 2025.
12. "South Africa." *Nairobi Convention*, n.d., nairobiconvention.org. Accessed 4 Feb. 2025.
13. "Lala Palm." *Siyabona Africa*, 2024, krugerpark.co.za. Accessed 4 Feb. 2025.
14. "Wild Date Palm." *Siyabona Africa*, 2024, krugerpark.co.za. Accessed 4 Feb. 2025.
15. Taylah Strauss. "Everything You Need to Know about the Clanwilliam Cedar Tree." *Getaway*, 21 June 2022, getaway.co.za. Accessed 4 Feb. 2025.
16. "African Protea." *San Diego Zoo Wildlife Alliance*, 2025, animals.sandiegozoo.org. Accessed 4 Feb. 2025.
17. "African Protea."
18. Daniel Koopowitz. "The Marine Big Five—South Africa's Icons of the Deep." *Ker Downey Africa*, 2025, ker-downeyafrica.com. Accessed 4 Feb. 2025.
19. "Sea Dwellers." *PBS*, n.d., pbs.org. Accessed 4 Feb. 2025.
20. Koopowitz, "The Marine Big Five."
21. Koopowitz, "The Marine Big Five."

CHAPTER 4. HISTORY

1. "Fossil Hominid Sites of South Africa." *UNESCO World Heritage Convention*, 2005, whc.unesco.org. Accessed 17 Feb. 2025.
2. "Fossil Hominid Sites of South Africa."
3. "The Khoikhoi." *Genadendal*, n.d., genadendal.info. Accessed 4 Feb. 2025.
4. "The Arrival of the Khoisan." *South African History Online*, 14 Oct. 2011, sahistory.org.za. Accessed 4 Feb. 2025.
5. Julian R. D. Cobbing and Colin J. Bundy. "History of South Africa." *Britannica*, 5 Feb. 2025, britannica.com. Accessed 5 Feb. 2025.
6. Cobbing and Bundy, "History of South Africa."
7. "South African War." *Britannica*, 21 Dec. 2024, britannica.com. Accessed 5 Feb. 2025.
8. "South Africa Act." *Britannica*, n.d., britannica.com. Accessed 5 Feb. 2025.
9. "Opposition to Apartheid." *Britannica*, 3 Feb. 2025, britannica.com. Accessed 5 Feb. 2025.
10. "Soweto Uprising, 1976." *Divestment for Humanity*, n.d., michiganintheworld.history.lsa.umich.edu. Accessed 5 Feb. 2025.
11. "Soweto Uprising, 1976."
12. "Truth and Reconciliation Commission." *Britannica*, 16 Dec. 2024, britannica.com. Accessed 5 Feb. 2025.
13. "Informal Housing, Poverty, and Legacies of Apartheid in South Africa." *Urban@UW*, 11 July 2019, urban.uw.edu. Accessed 5 Feb. 2025.

SOURCE **NOTES** CONTINUED

CHAPTER 5. PEOPLE AND CULTURE

1. "South Africa." *CIA World Factbook*, 24 Jan. 2025, cia.gov. Accessed 5 Feb. 2025.
2. "South Africa."
3. "Religions." *CIA World Factbook*, n.d., cia.gov. Accessed 5 Feb. 2025.
4. "South Africa." *Olympedia*, 2023, olympedia.org. Accessed 5 Feb. 2025.
5. "What Is Freedom Day in South Africa and Why Do We Celebrate It?" *African Travel Canvas*, 8 Mar. 2021, africantravelcanvas.com. Accessed 5 Feb. 2025.

CHAPTER 6. POLITICS

1. "The Structure of Government." *People's Assembly*, n.d., pa.org.za. Accessed 5 Feb. 2025.
2. Hassan Isilow. "South Africa Inaugurates New Cabinet in Government of National Unity." *Anadolu Agency*, 7 Mar. 2024, aa.com. Accessed 5 Feb. 2025.
3. Tannur Anders. "Which Parties Make Up South Africa's Unity Government?" *Reuters*, 24 June 2024, reuters.com. Accessed 5 Feb. 2025.
4. Anders, "Which Parties Make Up South Africa's Unity Government?"
5. Anders, "Which Parties Make Up South Africa's Unity Government?"
6. "Election Results and Allocation of Seats in Parliament (National Assembly) and Provincial Legislatures: 2024." *Parliamentary Monitoring Group*, 20 June 2024, pmg.org.za. Accessed 3 Mar. 2025.
7. "South Africa." *CIA World Factbook*, 24 Jan. 2025, cia.gov. Accessed 5 Feb. 2025.
8. "National Anthem." *South African Consulate General*, 2024, southafrica-usa.net. Accessed 5 Feb. 2025.
9. "National Anthem."

CHAPTER 7. ECONOMICS

1. Marcus Lu. "Mapped: Breaking Down the $3 Trillion African Economy by Country." *Visual Capitalist*, 5 Mar. 2024, visualcapitalist.com. Accessed 5 Feb. 2025.
2. "Gold in South Africa." *Observatory of Economic Complexity*, Oct. 2024, oec.world. Accessed 5 Feb. 2025.
3. "South Africa." *Observatory of Economic Complexity*, Oct. 2024, oec.world. Accessed 5 Feb. 2025.
4. "South Africa," *Observatory of Economic Complexity.*
5. "South Africa," *Observatory of Economic Complexity.*
6. Julian R. D. Cobbing and Colin J. Bundy. "Diamonds, Gold, and Imperialist Intervention (1870–1902)." *Britannica*, 5 Feb. 2025, britannica.com. Accessed 5 Feb. 2025.
7. Julian R. D. Cobbing and Colin J. Bundy. "South Africa." *Britannica*, 2 Mar. 2025, britannica.com. Accessed 3 Mar. 2025.
8. Natalie Cowling. "Tourism in South Africa." *Statista*, 16 Aug. 2024, statista.com. Accessed 5 Feb. 2025.
9. "Maloti-Drakensberg Park." *UNESCO World Heritage Convention*, n.d. whc.unesco.org. Accessed 4 Feb. 2025.
10. Randolph Vigne and Martin Hall. "South Africa." *Britannica*, 17 Feb. 2025, britannica.com. Accessed 17 Feb. 2025.
11. Vigne and Hall, "South Africa."
12. "2021 Insights into Car Ownership and Preferences across the African Continent." *Biz Community*, 14 Sept. 2021, bizcommunity.africa. Accessed 5 Feb. 2025.
13. Anton van Dalsen. "Minibus Taxis." *Helen Suzman Foundation*, 2025, hsf.org. Accessed 5 Feb. 2025.
14. James Barber, Angela Fung, et. al. "Telkom South Africa." *Emerging Markets Quarterly*, Winter 1999, people.duke.edu. Accessed 5 Feb. 2025.

15. "Convert 1,000 ZAR to USD." *Revolut*, n.d., revolut.com. Accessed 5 Feb. 2025.

16. Paula Gilbert. "Telkom SA Now Has Over 20M Mobile Subs." *Connecting Africa*, 19 June 2024, connectingafrica.com. Accessed 5 Feb. 2025.

17. "The World Bank in South Africa." *World Bank Group*, 4 Feb. 2025, worldbank.org. Accessed 5 Feb. 2025.

18. "The World Bank in South Africa."

19. Ray Mahlaka. "Transnet's Critical Operation and Financial Situation Extends from Bad to Worse." *Daily Maverick*, 2 Jan. 2024, dailymaverick.co.za. Accessed 3 Mar. 2025.

CHAPTER 8. SOUTH AFRICA TODAY

1. "Beaches in South Africa." *Where It All Began*, n.d., whereitallbegan.travel. Accessed 5 Feb. 2025.

2. Magdalena Laas. "The Education System in South Africa." *Expatica*, 4 Feb. 2025, expatica.com. Accessed 5 Feb. 2025.

3. Patricia Bauer. "Bantu Education Act." *Britannica*, n.d., britannica.com. Accessed 5 Feb. 2025.

4. "South African Private School Price Shocker." *Business Tech*, 30 May 2024, businesstech.co.za. Accessed 5 Feb. 2025.

5. Antony Sguazzin. "South Africa Wealth Gap Unchanged Since Apartheid, Says World Inequality Lab." *Time*, 5 Aug. 2021, time.com. Accessed 5 Feb. 2025.

6. Natalie Cowling. "Number of People Living in Extreme Poverty in South Africa from 2016–2030." *Statista*, 23 Oct. 2024. statista.com. Accessed 5 Feb. 2025.

7. "South African Unemployment Rate." *Trading Economics*, 2024, tradingeconomics.com. Accessed 5 Feb. 2025.

8. "South Africa Youth Unemployment Rate." *Trading Economics*, 2024, tradingeconomics.com. Accessed 5 Feb. 2025.

9. "What Share of South African Households Have Access to Electricity from the Grid?" *Africa Check*, 31 Jan. 2024, africacheck.org. Accessed 5 Feb. 2025.

10. Arwen Kozak. "Shedding the Load: Power Shortages Widen Divides in South Africa." *Kleinman Center for Energy Policy*, 28 July 2023, kleinmanenergy.upenn.edu. Accessed 5 Feb. 2025.

11. "Climate Risk Country Profile: South Africa." *World Bank Group*, 2021, climateknowledgeportal.worldbank.org. Accessed 5 Feb. 2025.

12. Natalie Cowling. "Provincial Household Access to Tap Water in South Africa 2022, by Type." *Statista*, 3 Dec. 2024, statista.com. Accessed 5 Feb. 2025.

13. David McKenzie and Sarah Dean. "'I Knew I Could Be Killed': This Cash Van Guard Is Just One of South Africa's Crime Wave Victims." *CNN*, 28 Mar. 2024, cnn.com. Accessed 5 Feb. 2025.

14. "As Police Lose the War on Crime In South Africa, Private Security Companies Step In." *NPR*, 7 Jan. 2024. npr.org. Accessed 5 Feb. 2025.

INDEX

NIGERIA

BY RACHEL BITHELL

Essential Library

An Imprint of Abdo Publishing
abdobooks.com

ABDOBOOKS.COM
Published by Abdo Publishing, a division of ABDO, PO Box 398166, Minneapolis, Minnesota 55439.

Printed in China.
052025
092025

Cover Photo: Shutterstock Images (main); Irina Sevostyanova/Shutterstock Images (pattern)
Interior Photos: Kehinde Temitope Odutayo/Shutterstock Images, 4–5; Paul Odijie/iStockphoto, 7; Johnny Greig/iStockphoto, 8; Shutterstock Images, 11, 18 (globe), 30, 31, 32, 36, 37, 39, 40–41, 45, 54, 57, 60, 61, 62, 63, 68, 76–77, 78, 80, 91, 101; Prachaya Roekdeethaweesab/Shutterstock Images, 12; David Havel/Shutterstock Images, 14; Amaka Chidioka/Shutterstock Images, 16–17; Red Line Editorial, 18 (map); Oni Abimbola/Shutterstock Images, 20, 95; Funmi Ajala/Shutterstock Images, 23; Fabian Plock/Shutterstock Images, 25; Iyke Oby/iStockphoto, 26–27; Martin Pelanek/Shutterstock Images, 28–29; Henner Damke/Shutterstock Images, 35; Wikimedia Commons, 43, 44; ilbusca/DigitalVision Vectors/Getty Images, 47; Express Newspapers/Archive Photos/Getty Images, 48; Helene C. Stikkel/US Department of Defense, 50; Agbebiyi Adekunle Sunday/Shutterstock Images, 52–53, 79; Tolu Owoeye/Shutterstock Images, 58, 73, 93; Ovinuchi Prince Ejiohuo/Wikimedia Commons, 66–67; Vic Josh/Shutterstock Images, 74; Richard Juilliart/Shutterstock Images, 82; iStockphoto, 85; Ajibola Fasola/Shutterstock Images, 88–89; Omotayo Kofoworola/Shutterstock Images, 92; Malte Ossowski/Sven Simon/picture-alliance/dpa/AP Images, 98

Editor: Kari Cornell
Series Designer: Maggie Villaume

Library of Congress Control Number: 2024948572

PUBLISHER'S CATALOGING-IN-PUBLICATION DATA
Names: Bithell, Rachel, author.
Title: Nigeria / by Rachel Bithell
Description: Minneapolis, Minnesota: Abdo Publishing, 2026 | Series: Essential library of countries | Includes online resources and index.
Identifiers: ISBN 9781098296995 (lib. bdg.) | ISBN 9798384919513 (ebook)
Subjects: LCSH: Geography--Juvenile literature. | Nigeria--Civilization--Juvenile literature. | Africa--Juvenile literature. | Nigeria--History--Juvenile literature.
Classification: DDC 966.9--dc23

CONTENTS

CHAPTER **ONE**

A TOUR OF NIGERIA

Alex and his mom were on a video call with his uncle, Ayo, at his home in Nigeria. But it was Ayo's baby's chubby cheeks and brown eyes that filled the screen. Alex wished he could meet his new cousin in person, but his mom said travel in Nigeria would be dangerous right now. At least Alex had memories and lots of pictures from visiting his uncle a couple of years before. When they finished the call, Alex pulled up those photos on the computer. Memories of that trip came flooding back.

Alex remembered that he and his mom had boarded a plane in Chicago and flown to Frankfurt, Germany. There was just enough time to grab lunch and change planes before taking off for Lagos, Nigeria,

The city of Lagos was built on Lagos Island, Iddo Island, Ikoyi Island, and Victoria Island.

the city in which his mother had grown up. As they flew in, Alex could see that the buildings of Nigeria's largest city stopped abruptly at the coast. Beyond, the blue waters of the Gulf of Guinea stretched to the horizon. The late afternoon sun reflecting off the ocean made a scene worthy of a postcard. Alex had snapped a picture from the plane.

A flight attendant announced that the local temperature was 31 degrees Celsius. Alex did a quick conversion on his phone—that was 88 degrees Fahrenheit.[1] It was much warmer than autumn in Illinois, where he lived. His phone had adjusted to local time, six hours later than back home. Alex had been traveling for almost 20 hours, with only a few hours of sleep on the plane. No wonder he felt so tired.

At the airport, his mom hailed a yellow, three-wheeled taxi called a *keke*. It was only a few miles to their hotel, but the keke made slow progress through the streets of Lagos. In the crush of cars, motorbikes, other kekes, and people, the traffic inched along. Outside the open taxi, skyscrapers filled the skyline.

THE GEOLOGY OF THE GULF OF GUINEA

South of Nigeria lies part of the Atlantic Ocean known as the Gulf of Guinea. The geology of the tectonic plate located under the gulf closely corresponds to that of the plate under Brazil's east coast. This evidence supports the current theory of continental drift, which says that Africa and South America were once both part of a supercontinent. The areas that are now Brazil and Nigeria were side by side until about 140 million years ago.

EXPLORING LAGOS

They were up early the next morning. Alex's mom said it was the best way to beat jet lag. A short walk

Lagos is known for having some of the worst traffic jams in the world. Those who drive in the city spend an average of three hours in traffic each day.

took them to a stop where they boarded a public bus bound for Lagos Island, a part of the city on an island in the Niger delta. The bus traveled in a dedicated lane, avoiding a huge traffic jam on the main road. Alex's mom called traffic jams "go-slows." Their fare was 500 naira each, about 30 US cents.[2]

From the bus stop, they walked to Freedom Park, the site of a prison during British colonial rule. In 2010 it had been converted to a park and museum to mark the fiftieth anniversary of Nigeria's independence from the United Kingdom. Alex took pictures of the beautiful gardens and the sculptures on display. Many depicted people engaged in traditional crafts and trades. Inside the museum, he saw the chains that had once bound political prisoners opposed to colonial rule. It was a bleak reminder of Nigeria's road to freedom.

Stalls at the Lekki Arts and Craft Market showcase the work of Nigerian artisans, including metalwork sculptures and handmade items decorated with elaborate beadwork.

Alex's mom used the Bolt app to book a car that took them to Lekki Arts and Crafts Market. First, they stopped for lunch at a nearby restaurant. Mom ordered fresh grilled corn, still on the cob, and *dundun*, a dish made from deep-fried yam. The dundun was sweet and savory at the same time. For dessert they had a sweet, deep-fried dough called puff puff.

After lunch, they strolled the rows of market stalls, which offered handmade jewelry, masks, drums, artwork, and so much more. Alex could have stayed for hours and not seen everything. He chose a colorful backpack he could use for the rest of their trip. He bargained with the friendly seller until the price dropped from 1,400 naira to 800 naira, or about 47 cents.[3] The seller bargained with Alex in English, but his mom was pleased that the man spoke to her in Yoruba, her first language.

STREET FOOD IN NIGERIA

The streets of Nigeria's large cities offer a diverse array of options for locals and travelers who want a quick meal. Many of the most popular choices are made from vegetables that reflect the staples of Nigerians' diets. For example, *abacha* is a salad made from cooked, shredded cassava root tossed with green vegetables, palm oil, and onions. Roasted ground peanuts are the main ingredient in *kulikuli*, a popular, crunchy snack. This peanut paste is often spiced with pepper or ginger, then formed into sticks or wafers and deep fried.

They spent the next day at the Lekki Conservation Centre. Its 193 acres (78 ha) of forest and mangrove swamp were almost hidden by the surrounding city until they passed through the entrance. Inside, they watched the wildlife from Africa's longest canopy walkway, a system of hanging walks and bridges more than 1,300 feet (400 m) long.[4] The crocodiles were impressive, but Alex liked watching the mona monkeys best. He even got some pictures of a couple of the lively creatures playing on the walkway. A guide told them flooding had become more of a threat to the center in recent years. Homes and businesses built around it interfered with the natural channels for runoff. During the rainy season, between March and November, the city received around 70 inches (178 cm) of rain.[5]

THE CAPITAL CITY

The next morning, they checked out of the hotel and headed back to the airport for the short flight to Abuja, Nigeria's capital city. The plane covered the 318 miles (512 km) in a little more than an hour.[6] Uncle Ayo worked for Nigeria's government and had moved there several years earlier. He met them at the airport, and after lots of hugs, they all hopped on the light rail train that took them into the city center.

In 2023 the population of Lagos was 15.95 million people, making it making it Africa's third-largest city.[7]

This city looked very different from Lagos. Ayo explained that the city had been planned and built starting in the 1980s, so its central area was less crowded than the older Lagos. The weather was less humid and a little cooler, too, which was good for sightseeing.

Over the next several days, they explored Abuja in Ayo's car, with Ayo serving as their guide and driver. At the National Children's Park and Zoo they saw hyenas, ostriches, and lions. From the

Aso Rock, located near Abuja, is 1,312 feet (400 m) tall.

small lake inside the park, they had a great view of Aso Rock, a huge land formation located to the north. Alex was so impressed that Ayo suggested they drive to see the massive Zuma Rock, which stands just outside of Abuja. Ayo said the rock rises 3,280 feet (1,000 m) above the surrounding landscape.[8] Alex got a great selfie in front of the imposing landmark.

On another afternoon, the family toured the National Mosque. Alex learned more about the history and influence of Islam in Nigeria. The mosque itself, with its stunning architecture and decoration, inspired quiet admiration.

Uncle Ayo was most excited about attending a football match at Moshood Abiola National Stadium in Abuja. He said the stadium could hold more than 60,000 people.[9] That made it about the same size as Soldier Field in Chicago, where Alex had once seen the Chicago Fire FC play. Back home, Alex and his friends called the sport soccer. He took lots of pictures to show his soccer teammates at school, hoping it would help make up for the game he was missing during his trip.

The home crowd was jubilant when Nigeria's Super Eagles defeated Benin's Les Guépards, or "the Cheetahs." The sea of people, many wearing green and white, cheered and waved flags. Alex took a video to capture the sound of the celebration. He was amazed by how excited and loud the crowd was.

ZUMA ROCK

One of the most famous landmarks in Nigeria, Zuma Rock, is an example of the inselbergs, or isolated large hills, that dot the central part of the country. The Zuba people, who believed the rock had spiritual significance, settled around Zuma Rock beginning in the 1400s. The impressive hill has become a symbol of Nigeria. Between 1999 and 2014, an image of Zuma Rock was featured on the nation's money.

KAINJI LAKE NATIONAL PARK

The final destination of their trip was Kainji Lake National Park. A long day of driving took them 310 miles (500 km) through the grassy steppes and savannas.[10] Trees dotted the otherwise open landscape. The next morning, Alex was eager to board the boat that would give them a tour of the lake. His mom explained that they wouldn't see all the lake's 500 square miles (1,300 sq km).[11]

It was too big for one tour. Still, the wide-open water reminded him a little bit of Lake Michigan back home.

But there was nothing in Lake Michigan that came even close to hippopotamuses. The boat operator gave them a wide berth, explaining that the animals would be aggressive if they felt threatened. Hippos can weigh as much as 3,000 pounds (1,360 kg) and are armed with tusks more than a foot (0.3 m) long.[12] The animals are more dangerous to humans than crocodiles or lions are. Alex had to zoom in to get some great pictures. In one, a hippo seemed to be yawning widely, showing its impressive canine teeth.

There was so much to see around the lake that they spent the next few days hiking and watching wildlife. On a guided hike, Alex learned the park was home to more than 350 species of birds, including the secretary bird, which Alex thought looked like an odd cross between a chicken and a roadrunner.[13] Later in the hike, they spotted a leopard. It appeared to be on the hunt for its next meal. The guide let Alex use his binoculars to get a better view of the big cat through the tall grass while they kept a safe distance.

Alex was a little sad as he viewed the final pictures from their trip. After driving back to Abuja, Uncle Ayo had taken them to the airport, where they would retrace their path to get home, flying first to Lagos, then stopping over in Europe before the final flight to Chicago. In the last picture, Alex stood between his smiling mom and her brother outside the light rail station. Since then, Uncle Ayo had married and now had a baby. Alex hoped he would someday have a picture of the whole family.

Hippos can stay underwater without needing to breathe for as long as five minutes.

A DIVERSE COUNTRY

Hundreds of ethnic groups call Nigeria home, each adding its own unique culture to Nigeria's heritage. Nigeria's music, dance, food, and art have traditions going back hundreds if not thousands of years. Many people who live in Nigeria speak two or three languages, including a traditional language of their ethnic group as well as Nigeria's official language, English.

Nigeria is also rich in natural beauty, with ecosystems that include coastal swamps, rainforests, savannas, and deserts. Its wildlife includes species recognized around the world, such as lions, hippopotamuses, and elephants. Nigeria is also a global hot spot for biodiversity in both the plant and animal kingdoms. The country has abundant natural resources, including petroleum and natural gas and minerals such as tin and columbite.

WORKING FOR A BRIGHTER FUTURE

Despite these advantages, Nigeria struggles with serious political, economic, and environmental challenges. The country's ethnic groups were brought together by colonialism rather than a shared identity. Deep divisions between ethnic and religious groups continue to cause conflicts. Decades of colonial rule planted seeds of corruption and instability that have challenged the Nigerian government since the country gained its independence in 1960. Poor governance has also contributed to widespread poverty and unemployment. The mismanagement of land and climate change are turning some of Nigeria's land to desert and subjecting other areas to devastating floods.

These are daunting problems. Yet many Nigerians, especially those of younger generations, remain hopeful. They still work for a brighter future, with the hope of changing the course of their country. Through education and activism, they are tackling the difficult issues facing their nation.

CHAPTER **TWO**

GEOGRAPHY

Nigeria is a country in western Africa. It is part of a region known as sub-Saharan Africa. This is the area south of the Sahara desert, which includes several African nations. All of Nigeria is north of the equator. Nigeria is a large country, about twice the size of California. With about 237 million people, Nigeria is the most populous country in Africa and the sixth-most populated country in the world.[1]

In the south, Nigeria borders the Gulf of Guinea, which is part of the Atlantic Ocean. It has 530 miles (853 km) of coastline along its southern shore.[2] To the west, Nigeria borders Benin. The country of Niger lies to its north. Both Chad and Cameroon border Nigeria to the east.

The country is divided into 36 states. Lagos State in the southeast is home to the city of Lagos. It is the

Idanre Hill, located in the southwestern Nigerian state of Ondo, rises 3,000 feet (914 m) above sea level.

MAP OF NIGERIA

KEY:

- Capital
- City
- Point of Interest

country's most populated state and most important economic center. In the central part of Nigeria, Plateau State, which includes the city of Jos, is a center for mining. To the northeast, Bauchi State is home to a large national park that preserves some of Nigeria's savannas, areas of grassy plains with scattered trees. In the far northeast, Borno State borders Lake Chad. The southeastern state of Cross River is sparsely populated and has become an important center for conservation efforts. The Federal Capital Territory near the center of the country is an independent political entity that is home to the national government. Much like Washington, DC, it is not part of a state. It is an independent region within Nigeria.

REGIONS OF NIGERIA

The Niger delta is the most prominent geographic feature in the southern part of Nigeria. Deltas are low wetlands that form when rivers empty into a large body of water, usually an ocean. Over millions of years, sediment carried by the river builds up at its mouth, pushing the shoreline farther into the ocean. Like other deltas, the Niger delta's landmasses are separated by narrow channels of water. Nigeria's lowest elevation is its sea-level coastline along the Atlantic. Several islands off Nigeria's southern coast are also part of the country. These include Adoni Island, Banana Island, and Bonny Island.

The Niger delta covers about 13,900 square miles (36,000 sq km).[3]

The city of Lagos is situated on the coast to the west of the delta. It straddles several islands

The small-scale fishers who work the waters of the Niger delta are key to meeting the food demands of a growing Nigerian population.

and isthmuses, including Lagos Island and the Lekki Isthmus, which are surrounded by lagoons. The lagoons and the river delta are swampy and prone to flooding during seasons of heavy rain. Flooding is a perennial problem in Lagos and the coastal cities of the Niger delta.

The central part of Nigeria features hills and plateaus with wide valleys between them. Much of this landscape was created by ancient volcanoes, which made landforms that have since been eroded. Inselbergs, for example, such as Zuma Rock, are large, rocky hills that jut above the surrounding landscape. Zuma Rock is 3,280 feet (1,000 m) tall.[4] The underlying rock is largely igneous and is older and harder than the sedimentary rock below the delta region. Igneous rock forms when lava or magma cools and solidifies. Especially beneath the Jos Plateau, this rock contains several valuable minerals such as tin and columbite.

Along the border with Cameroon to the southeast, Nigeria is mountainous. The area is known as the Cameroon Highlands and includes the Gotel and the Shebshi mountain ranges. Nigeria's highest points are Chappal Waddi at 7,936 feet (2,419 m) in the Gotel Mountains and Mount Dimlang at 6,699 feet (2,042 m) in the Shebshi Mountains.[5]

Vast plains cover the northern part of Nigeria. This area, known as the Sahel region, forms a transition between the Sahara to the north and more humid areas to the south. Since the late 1900s, the area has become more arid and lost some of its vegetation, especially near the northern border. Through this process, known as desertification, the Sahara is encroaching into Nigeria.

NIGERIA'S COASTAL CITIES

The coastline is the most densely populated area of Nigeria. Its port cities have been important centers of sea trading for centuries. Revenue from industries centered in Lagos and oil production, both inland and offshore, make the coast the backbone of Nigeria's economy. However, mismanagement of resources and poorly planned development have impoverished many of its residents and created environmental problems such as poor sanitation, pollution, and flooding.

WATERWAYS

Nigeria derives its name from the Niger River, which is the third-longest river in Africa. The Niger River enters the country in the northwest where Nigeria's border meets Niger and Benin. It runs southeast before turning south and emptying into the Gulf of Guinea. Traveling or shipping by boat on the Niger River has historically been difficult. This is due to seasonal flooding and the river's many rapids and waterfalls, especially along its course through the central plateaus. However, several dam projects have helped make the river more navigable.

The Benue River is a major tributary of the Niger. It enters the country along the eastern border with Cameroon and runs west before joining the Niger. The Benue is relatively calm and easy to navigate, but some areas become too shallow in the dry season for commercial boats.

In the northeastern part of the country, rivers flow toward Lake Chad rather than the Atlantic Ocean. Lake Chad is located where the borders of Chad, Cameroon, Niger, and Nigeria meet. In this semiarid area, the lake has been a vital water source for people and wildlife for centuries, including as an important stop on trans-Saharan trade routes. The Jama'are and Komadugu Yobe Rivers are among the larger rivers that drain into Lake Chad.

In the far eastern part of Nigeria, the Cross River runs north to south. The river empties into the Gulf of Guinea through an estuary that is shared with the Calabar River. The Cross River provides drainage for the rainforest in the wettest part of the country and is an important waterway for shipping.

UDI-NSUKKA PLATEAU

The eastern edges of the Nsukka Plateau and Udi Plateau are known as the Udi-Nsukka Plateau. Part of the central plateau region, the escarpment forms sheer cliffs with an average elevation of about 1,000 feet (300 m). The highest point is nearly twice that elevation, 1,897 feet (578 m).[6] The escarpment is famous for its stunning views, including of numerous waterfalls formed as tributaries of the Cross River and Niger River tumble over its edge.

The water flowing over the Matsirga Waterfalls in Nigeria's Kaduna State plunges 98 feet (30 m) into the pool below.

Nigeria is also home to several large reservoirs created by dam projects along its rivers. Kainji Lake was created in 1968 by damming the Niger River in western Nigeria on the border between Niger State and Kebbi State. In northwestern Nigeria, along the Sokoto River, the Bakolori Dam was completed in 1978, creating the lake of the same name. In addition to providing flood control, these lakes are important for wildlife, irrigation, and fishing.

THE SHRINKING LAKE CHAD

Climate change and poor land management are shrinking Lake Chad. The lake has previously covered as much as 6,875 square miles (17,800 sq km), but in the 2000s and 2010s, its area averaged only about 580 square miles (1,500 sq km). Plants and animals are losing habitat. Increased competition between fishers, farmers, and herders who rely on the lake has led to violence. The humanitarian organization Refugees International estimates that three million people have been displaced due to drought and conflict in the area.[9]

NIGERIA'S CLIMATE

All of Nigeria has a warm climate with dry and rainy seasons, but temperatures and rainfall vary significantly across the country. In the south, the rainy season lasts from March through November. The southeast is the wettest part of the country, receiving about 120 inches (305 cm) of rain per year. The southwest receives about 70 inches (178 cm) of annual rainfall.[7]

Nigeria's southern coast is warm year-round, with little variation in temperature. For example, in Lagos, the warmest months are January and February, which have average high temperatures of about 88 degrees Fahrenheit (31°C). In the coolest months of July and August, the average high temperature is about 80 degrees Fahrenheit (27°C).[8] The coast is swampy, and mangrove forests hug the shoreline where they have not been cleared for development or killed by oil spills. Farther inland are freshwater swamps, which give way to tropical rainforests to the north. Much of the natural rainforest has been replaced by tropical agricultural plants such as oil palm, rubber, and cacao trees.

North of the rainforest belt, the central portion of the country receives less rain and has more variation in temperature. Abuja, located in the center of the country, receives around 58 inches (147 cm) of rain annually. Its average monthly high temperature is 96 degrees Fahrenheit (36°C) in March but 79 degrees Fahrenheit (26°C) in August.[10] The wide plateaus and valleys of this region are mostly savannas.

The Sahel region in the north is hot and dry. To the northwest lie the Sokoto Plains, while the Borno Plains occupy the northeast. In the

In southwestern Nigeria, rainforests grow along the Niger delta and in the Nigerian Lowland Forest ecosystem.

A bird's-eye view of northeastern Nigeria's Borno State shows the arid, unpopulated Sahel region.

far northeast, the city of Maiduguri has average high temperatures that range between about 87 and 104 degrees Fahrenheit (31°C and 40°C). The rainy season is shorter, lasting from mid-May to September. During that time, the city receives almost all its annual precipitation of about 20 to 22 inches (51–56 cm).[11] Vegetation becomes sparser as the grasslands merge with the Sahara in the north.

The harmattan is a cool, dry wind that blows from the Sahara across Nigeria from late November to mid-March. It has the greatest impact in the Sahel region but also influences the climate of the central plateaus and, to a lesser degree, the coast. It contributes to drier weather and more temperature variability. During this season, nighttime temperatures in the northeast can be cool enough to produce frost.

CHAPTER **THREE**

PLANTS AND ANIMALS

Due to its warm climate and diverse habitats, Nigeria has historically been a hot spot for plant and animal biodiversity. Many of Africa's most recognized animal species once inhabited its waters, jungles, and grasslands. The rainforest supported red river hogs, forest elephants, and chimpanzees. Antelopes, hyenas, lions, baboons, and giraffes roamed the savanna. Leopards, golden cats, monkeys, gorillas, and wild pigs moved between both areas. Crocodiles and hippos populated Nigeria's lakes and rivers.

Since the early 1900s, Nigeria's growing population has created a demand for more agriculture to feed its people. Large portions of the rainforest and savanna

Chimpanzees still live in the rainforests that extend along the border between Nigeria and Cameroon.

Hartebeests, which means "deer beast" in Dutch, are large antelopes that roam the Yankari Game Reserve in eastern Nigeria.

have been cleared for farming food crops, converted to commercial crops such as rubber and cacao, or overgrazed by livestock. As a result, species have suffered habitat loss, and some animals, such as lions and elephants, are now found only in protected areas. Others, such as rhinoceroses and giraffes, no longer live in Nigeria.

NATIONAL PARKS

Nigeria's conservation programs for wildlife are centered on its national parks. Yankari National Park (YNP) in Bauchi State is also known as Yankari Game Reserve. It is home to some of the country's most treasured wildlife. Its 866 square miles (2,244 sq km) support between 100 and 150 savanna elephants, the largest surviving elephant population in Nigeria. YNP is also home to one of only four known populations of the critically endangered West African lion.[1] Hippopotamuses, buffalo, hartebeests, and roan antelope also inhabit the park. The diverse animal life makes it a popular destination for wildlife viewing, and the park offers organized safaris.

Conservation efforts at YNP have often met with resistance from surrounding communities, whose residents largely rely on subsistence farming for their livelihood. Some farmers see the animals of the preserve as competition for resources such as water and pastureland, and they may illegally graze or water their livestock within the park. Many locals also view the wild predators on the reserve, such as lions, as a threat to their herds. At the same time, illegal hunting has reduced wild animal populations as hunters target the animals for meat or for pelts, teeth, bones, or ivory, which have value on the black market.

Since 2014, Bauchi State and the Wildlife Conservation Society (WCS) have co-managed YNP. Improved protections for wildlife include aerial patrols to monitor the movements of wildlife and detect poachers. Radio collars are being used to track elephant populations. In addition, officials are focusing on building better relationships with

HUMANS AND ELEPHANTS LIVING SIDE BY SIDE

As human populations increase and elephant habitats shrink, elephants and humans have more contact. Elephants and people often compete for scarce water, and roaming herds may eat or trample crops. Elephants that feel threatened sometimes attack people. Illegal poaching for meat or ivory is a source of income for people living in poverty. Preserving elephant populations will require supporting the well-being of the people who live side by side with them.

Cross River gorillas are considered critically endangered. Habitat loss, hunting, and disease threaten their survival.

neighboring communities and educating the public about the economic value of the animals. Elephants and other rare or popular wildlife attract tourists, who spend money in the local economy. Education programs also aim to teach people about the positive environmental impact of the park's wild plants and animals.

Cross River National Park (CRNP), located in Cross River State along the border with Cameroon, is another refuge for Nigeria's wildlife. Its 1,158 square miles (3,000 sq km) are home to the largest remaining tract of rainforest in Nigeria.[2] As such, it is an important center of biodiversity for both plants and animals. It supports a population of forest elephants, as well as leopards and chimpanzees. CRNP is the only place in Nigeria where the Preuss's red colobus and crested mona monkey are still found.

The Cross River gorilla, the world's most endangered great ape, lives in only small areas of the Cameroon Highlands, including parts of CRNP and protected areas across the border in Cameroon. The gorilla was identified by scientists in 1904 based on examples of skulls found in the Cross River region. In the 1970s, after a civil war in Nigeria, scientists feared these gorillas might be extinct, but expeditions in the 1980s found several surviving groups. According to the Cross River Gorilla Programme, fewer than 300 of these animals survive in the wild.[3]

In efforts to preserve the wildlife native to this part of Africa, the United Nations Educational, Scientific and Cultural Organization (UNESCO) has proposed forming a large protected area that would encompass CRNP. The proposed preserve would also incorporate Korup National Park in Cameroon and several smaller forests and preserves in both countries. The entire project would cover 5,400 square miles (14,000 sq km), an area larger than the state of Connecticut.[4]

WILDLIFE ACROSS NIGERIA

Even outside of protected areas, Nigeria is home to diverse plant and animal species. Rodents such as squirrels, porcupines, and cane rats are common. The African brush-tailed porcupine weighs about 6.6 pounds (3 kg) and is widely hunted for meat in both rural and urban areas.[5] Cane rats

Carpet viper bites kill about 10 percent of untreated victims. They bite thousands of people each year, killing the most people of any snake species in the world.[12]

may weigh up to 15 pounds (6.8 kg) and are also an important source of protein for people in the nation.[6]

Birds are abundant in Nigeria. Of more than 1,000 species, guinea fowl, quail, kites, vultures, and parrots are some of the most common.[7] A few of the world's birds are found only in Nigeria. One of these is the Jos Plateau indigobird. Males of the species are black with a blue-green sheen, while females are mottled shades of brown and gray. More brightly colored are the Rock firefinch, whose breast and shoulders are bright red, and the Anambra waxbill, with a rusty-colored breast and bright orange beak.

Nigeria is home to more than 100 species of reptiles.[8] Crocodiles inhabit rivers and lakes, and several snake species are found in various habitats in Nigeria. Some are venomous, including the puff adder, the boomslang, and three species of cobra. One, the black-necked spitting cobra, can eject its venom as far as 23 feet (7 m).[9] Nigeria's deadliest snake, the carpet viper, causes victims to bleed to death. Dunger's file snake, a black snake with rough scales, is found only in Nigeria. The Ondo forest gecko is found only in a small range in Ondo State in the southeastern part of the country.

About 20,000 species of insects inhabit Nigeria.[10] Roughly 1,000 of those species are butterflies living in Cross River State, including in the CRNP.[11] A rich variety of dragonflies, damselflies, and other insects also live in the state. Some, such as Gambles's flatwing damselfly, face extinction.

The African Grey Parrot is native to Africa, but populations in many nations, including Nigeria, are declining. Groups are capturing the birds to sell as pets.

Across Nigeria, mosquitoes are responsible for the transmission of malaria. The disease is caused by a parasite that is transferred from person to person through mosquito bites. Its symptoms include fever, chills, and vomiting, and it can be fatal. The World Health Organization estimated 68 million Nigerians contracted the disease and 194,000 died from it in 2021 alone, making it a major public health concern.[13]

PLANTS OF NIGERIA

Nigeria's vegetation, like its climate, follows geographic patterns. Along its coast, Nigeria is home to the largest mangrove forest in Africa and the third largest in the world. Mangroves grow only

Mangrove forests, including those along the Niger River in southern Nigeria, are among the most threatened habitats in the world.

in tropical habitats where fresh water meets salt water, usually where a river empties into an ocean, such as along the Niger delta. These forests make up less than 1 percent of the world's tropical forests but perform vital functions in the environment.[14] They provide shelter for fish and invertebrates throughout their life cycles. Mangroves also prevent erosion of the coastline, providing a buffer against damage from storms.

Just inland from the coast grows a band of tropical rainforest. Common native trees in the region include the tola and the okan. Both make up the forest's canopy, growing more than 164 feet (50 m) tall.[15] Oil palms are also indigenous to Nigeria's rainforests. These trees are valued for the oil that is harvested from their fruits. Large swaths of the rainforest have been converted to commercial plantations that grow oil palm, rubber, and cacao trees. Cacao trees grow beans that are made into products such as chocolate and cocoa butter. The cacao and rubber trees, originally from South America, were introduced to Nigeria in the late 1800s by European colonists.

In the middle of the country, savanna grasses and scattered trees dominate the landscape. One type of tree, the African baobab, has a distinctive shape with a wide trunk and twisted, spreading branches. The tamarind tree, also found on the savanna, is a hardy species that can grow in many types of soil and withstand drought. Known locally as *tsamiya*, its fruits have been valued by people across Nigeria for centuries.

In the Sahel region in the north, trees are mostly absent. The grasses of this region, such as Indian sandbur, are mostly short, annual species that provide forage for farmers' herds. A few shrubs, such as acacia, can also grow here. Even these hardy plants become sparse as the savanna transitions to the Sahara.

TAMARIND'S CULTURAL SIGNIFICANCE

Tamarind has been growing in Nigeria for centuries. Its fruit, which grows in curved brown pods, can be made into a tangy paste or juice. In many traditional cuisines of Nigeria's people, tamarind is a common and nutritious ingredient. It is also used in ceremonies and is a symbol of hospitality. For these reasons, tamarind has come to represent Nigeria's traditional cultures.

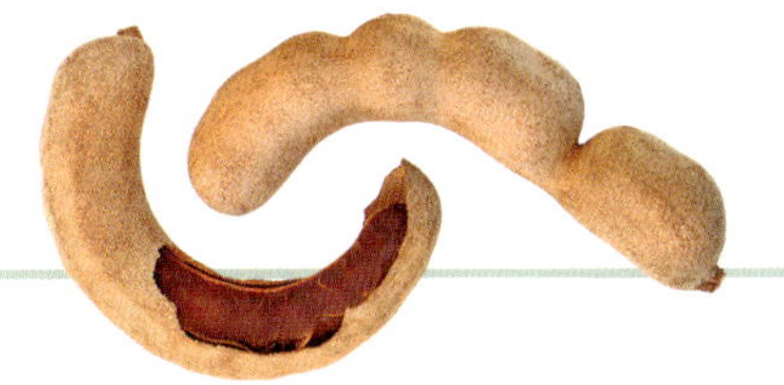

CONSERVATION EFFORTS IN NIGERIA

Efforts to protect Nigeria's native plants and animals are growing, but conservation programs face many challenges. Due to population growth and the mismanagement of land, Nigeria has difficulty producing enough food to feed its people, and huge tracts of wildland have been converted to farmland. In populous areas, natural landscapes have also been cleared to make way for housing and industry. Nigeria's economy relies heavily on oil production, and frequent spills and leaks have damaged surrounding ecosystems.

Since Nigeria's independence in 1960, the country's government has experienced instability and widespread corruption. Terrorism and violence between ethnic and religious groups often make areas of Nigeria dangerous. These factors have hindered efforts to protect the environment by the Nigerian government and private organizations operating within the country.

Still, many groups remain dedicated to conservation, with the most successful efforts centered on the country's state and national parks and preserves. Government agencies work with nonprofit groups and experts from around the world to preserve many of Nigeria's natural ecosystems. For example, the WCS partners with the government to run national parks.

In 2015, when the Nigerian president proposed a plan for a six-lane highway that would run through the heart of CRNP, the WCS and CRNP

HIGH AMBITION COALITION FOR NATURE AND PEOPLE

Nigeria is a member of the international organization High Ambition Coalition for Nature and People, whose goal is to place 30 percent of the world's land and oceans in protected parks and preserves by 2030. In 2023 about 10 percent of Nigeria's land area was protected, and the country was unlikely to meet the goal.[16] The same year, the government made some progress when Nigeria's National Assembly authorized the creation of ten new national parks. However, much of the land to be included in the new parks already had protected status. Some parcels of land were parts of state parks, for example.

staff led efforts to halt the project. In 2017, the government agreed to move the highway to the edge of the park. Yet by 2022, the government had decided to reject plans to reroute the highway. Both the highway and feeder roads threaten to destroy Nigeria's last remaining tropical rainforest.

Despite this major setback, in 2022 the nonprofit WildAid launched a huge media campaign to educate Nigerians about the value of conserving native wildlife. Aided by government officials, they broadcast and printed slogans such as "Keep them wild. Keep us safe" and "Poaching steals from us all" around the country.[17] Similar efforts in other countries have been effective in conserving threatened species.

Baobab trees are giant succulents that thrive in arid environments by absorbing water during the rainy season.

CHAPTER **FOUR**

HISTORY

The early history of human settlement in Nigeria is not well understood because archaeological studies in Nigeria are sparse. However, some evidence shows human activity in the country dates to tens of thousands of years ago. An archaeological site known as Ugwuelle-Uturu is thought to be an ancient location where tools were manufactured from local stone.

Excavations conducted in the area in 1977 and 1981 found thousands of stone axes, scrapers, knives, and other artifacts that are at least 90,000 years old. Some experts believe the site may be much older. The earliest known fossilized human remains in Nigeria come from an archaeological site called Iwo Eleru and date to 9000 BCE. Evidence and records of more recent human communities are more complete.

Artifacts from Nigerian civilizations were plundered by European colonizers. The Benin Bronzes, which date from the 1500s, were displayed at the British Museum in 2022.

FROM EARLY CULTURES THROUGH 1800

The earliest known culture in Nigeria belonged to the Nok. They lived on the plateaus of what is now central Nigeria in and around the city of Jos. Their culture dates to at least 500 BCE but may have been well established as early as 900 BCE. The Nok survived until about 200 CE. Evidence suggests their society was highly developed, with artisans, an organized religion, and iron smelting technology. They are known for their advanced terra-cotta sculptures, which often depicted stylized faces and figures. Modern art in Nigeria still shows influences from these sculptures.

For most of the past 1,000 years, many small states formed by ethnic groups covered what is now Nigeria. For example, ancestors of the Kanuri people formed a kingdom around the 800s CE in the Lake Chad region in both present-day Chad and Nigeria. In the Kanuri political system, the monarchs were men, but the king's mother had significant influence and women could hold government positions.

To the west, the Hausa people formed more than a dozen small city-states, each ruled by a monarch. These states vied with each other for control of trade routes and resources in the

ARCHAEOLOGY IN NIGERIA

Archaeologists in Nigeria contend with several challenges. The climate often makes it difficult to conduct digs. Many remote areas are inaccessible due to a lack of roads or roads that are poorly maintained. Political unrest and violence sometimes make parts of the country unsafe. Corrupt or ineffective governments prevent access to important sites. Dig sites may be looted by people looking to sell artifacts. Finally, acidic soils often degrade the condition of buried artifacts.

arid Sahel. The traditional religions of both the Kanuri and the Hausa included belief in multiple deities and nature spirits.

Beginning around the 1000s, traders from North Africa brought Islam to the Kanuri. By the 1300s, Islam was spreading among the Hausa as well. For many centuries, the practice of traditional religions mixed with Islam.

In the central part of Nigeria, the Yoruba people formed several small kingdoms representing sub-ethnic groups. These kingdoms all worshipped several deities. One of these gods, Ifa, was revered as the god of wisdom who taught humans a system of divination to help them know the will of the gods. In the 1000s, the kingdom of Ile-Ife became the most prominent in the region. In the 1300s, it was surpassed by the Oyo Empire.

Beginning in the 1200s, the Edo kingdom of Benin ruled the area around what is currently

Nok terra-cotta sculptures are all made using clay from the same source. They have been found in an area that covers 30,116 square miles (78,000 sq km).

Benin City in south-central Nigeria. This culture is known for its advanced brass sculptures, ivory, and wood carvings. In the south, the people of the Niger delta and Cross River areas did not form centralized governments. They include the ancestors of the Igbo and Ijo peoples.

The practice of slavery was somewhat common in these early kingdoms. Members of rival ethnic groups would capture and enslave each other during conflicts. However, slavery's scale and reach exploded after the arrival of Europeans in the late 1400s.

Portuguese explorers were the first Europeans to arrive in what is now Nigeria. They sailed first to the Niger delta and established trade with the Kingdom of Benin, including the slave trade. The English, Spanish, and Dutch soon joined the Portuguese in exploiting the people of West Africa. Experts estimate that around 3.5 million enslaved Africans departed from

The Benin Bronze cast relief plaques depict interactions between the Benin people and Europeans, including trade and battles to expand the Benin Empire.

Captured Africans were packed below deck for the trip to the Americas. Prior to 1750, one out of five Africans died on these ships due to starvation, disease, and poor treatment.

Nigeria's coasts as captives between about 1480 and 1840.[1] Some were taken to Europe, but most were sold to landowners in European colonies in the Caribbean and North and South America.

The impact of the slave trade to the area that would become Nigeria was devastating. Slave traders captured young, healthy people, leaving behind children and the elderly, who struggled to survive without able-bodied adults. Some local economies and cultures collapsed. Efforts to capture and enslave more people led to increased violence by Europeans and between Indigenous groups as many Nigerian kingdoms cooperated with European slave traders. The leaders of these kingdoms hoped to escape slavery themselves or to make money from it.

JIHAD AND COLONIZATION

By 1800, Islam had been slowly spreading through Nigeria for more than 500 years, especially among the upper classes of the Sahel region in the north. In part because Islamic law forbade Muslims from enslaving other Muslims, many people converted to Islam during the era of the slave trade. Usman dan Fodio was a prominent Muslim leader and scholar of the Fulani, a people who came to northern Nigeria from Senegal in the 1500s. Usman, as he is now called, wanted to eliminate elements of traditional religions from the practice of Islam. After recruiting enslaved people and those of the lower classes, he led a jihad against the rulers of many of Nigeria's kingdoms beginning in 1804. A jihad is a war against forces that oppose the Muslim faith.

At least 12 million Africans were enslaved throughout the continent between the 1400s and the 1800s.[2]

Within about four years, Usman had conquered much of the northern and central territories. Along with his son and his brother, he established a caliphate with its capital in the new city of Sokoto. A caliphate is an area ruled by a Muslim political and religious leader. Pressure from the caliphate and internal strife led to the collapse of the Oyo Empire in the 1830s. This ongoing instability led to conflicts among the Yoruba people in the central part of Nigeria.

Meanwhile, Britain had abolished the slave trade in 1807. During the Fulani jihad and Yoruba conflicts, many prisoners of war were enslaved. This fueled the slave trade at a time when Britain was trying to end it. Many companies from Britain wanted to build new trading relationships with former slave trade partners. Christian missionaries from Britain, largely motivated by abolitionism, entered Nigeria in greater numbers. These interests led to greater British involvement in Nigeria, including pushing farther into its interior.

In 1851, Britain shelled the city of Lagos with artillery as part of an effort to suppress the slave trade. In 1861, Britain annexed the city as a colony. Colonial rule spread from there, culminating with British victories over Benin in 1897 and Sokoto in 1903. The British divided the area into administrative areas called protectorates. In 1914, the Protectorate

Led by Captain George Charles Chardin Denton, the British annexed the land held by the king of Ado along the southern coast of Nigeria in 1891.

Nigerians celebrated their independence from the United Kingdom with sporting events and folk dancing in Enjugu, Nigeria, on October 11, 1960.

of Southern Nigeria was merged with the Protectorate of Northern Nigeria, creating Nigeria's present-day boundaries.

Britain, by now known as the United Kingdom, largely left local government to Indigenous political structures while retaining national control. In some cases, British leaders fueled conflict among ethnic groups to prevent any one group from threatening their power. During the colonial period, Christianity, the English language, and Western-style education spread in southern Nigeria. In the north, Nigeria's majority-Muslim regions resisted these influences, further dividing the north from the south. The British also encouraged growing cash crops. This practice prompted many people to migrate from existing settlements to agricultural areas.

During the early 1900s, opposition to colonial rule grew in many parts of Africa, including Nigeria. The democratic ideals promoted by the United Kingdom and the United States during

World War I (1914–1918) and World War II (1939–1945) helped bolster this opposition. Nigeria gained independence from the United Kingdom on October 1, 1960, in a peaceful transfer of power.

INDEPENDENT NIGERIA

Nigeria's initial constitution established a democratic government with an elected prime minister, a role first held by Abubakar Tafawa Balewa. Ethnic and regional conflicts and election fraud caused a crisis in January 1966 when Major General Johnson Aguiyi-Ironsi led a military coup and gained control of Nigeria. After just six months, Aguiyi-Ironsi was assassinated. The following year, three states in the east of the country declared independence. The resulting civil war lasted until 1970. The eastern separatists were defeated, and the three states remained part of Nigeria. Military rule continued.

In 1976, Olusegun Obasanjo came to power. Initially the leader of a military regime, Obasanjo committed to a return to civilian rule. A presidential election was held in 1979, and Obasanjo handed power over to the election's winner, Shehu Shagari. However, on New Year's Eve 1983, another coup brought back military rule. Ten years later, General Sani Abacha seized control of Nigeria and ruled as a dictator. He ignored the rule of law, persecuted the press, violated human rights, and used violence to suppress his critics until his death in 1998.

Abacha's death paved the way for a return of democracy. Elections were held, and Obasanjo won the presidency in 1999 and again in 2003. Limited to two terms, Obasanjo was succeeded by Umaru Musa Yar'Adua in 2007. When Yar'Adua died in 2010, his vice president, Goodluck Jonathan, succeeded him. Jonathan won reelection in 2011.

MINI **BIO**

OLUSEGUN OBASANJO

Born in 1937 in Abeokuta, Nigeria, Olusegun Obasanjo was from a Yoruba family. He attended a Christian high school and worked as a teacher before joining Nigeria's army in 1958. As the leader of a commando unit during Nigeria's civil war, he was the authority who accepted the surrender of the separatists in 1970. He was serving as a deputy to the leader of Nigeria's military government when that leader was assassinated in 1976. Over the next three years, Obasanjo oversaw the transition to a civilian government and democratic elections. In 1979, he stepped aside after the election, making him the first military leader in Africa to relinquish power to an elected government.

Over the next 15 years, Obasanjo ran a farm but remained active in several international groups, including working for the United Nations. He was a vocal critic of the military regimes that ruled Nigeria from 1983 to 1998. In 1995, dictator Sani Abacha had him jailed. Obasanjo was released in 1998 after Abacha's death.

The following year, Obasanjo won the election that marked Nigeria's return to democracy. During his two terms, supporters praised his economic reforms that led to growth and his fight against corruption. Critics said that his fight focused only on his opponents and that he was ineffective in resolving religious and ethnic tensions.

Olusegun Obasanjo, who was of Yoruba descent, served as the fifth and twelfth president of Nigeria.

KEN SARO-WIWA

Ken Saro-Wiwa was a Nigerian writer of plays, novels, poetry, and children's stories. He was also a critic of dictator Sani Abacha. In 1994, four chiefs who supported Abacha were murdered at a political rally, and Saro-Wiwa was charged with having a role in the murders. He was tried by three judges appointed by Abacha, convicted, and hanged. The event brought condemnation from leaders around the world and fueled opposition to Abacha's government.

The Islamic terrorist group Boko Haram gained prominence in 2009 and expanded its influence during Jonathan's rule. Boko Haram controlled large territories in Borno State. From there and other bases, the group targeted Christian schools, churches, and police and government buildings across the northeastern and central states, killing thousands of people.

The government was not able to control the violence. This contributed to Jonathan's defeat by Muhammad Buhari in 2015. Buhari served two terms. During that time, Nigeria grappled with a recession and continued ethnic and religious conflict. In 2023, Bola Tinubu won the presidential election against two other main candidates. During his campaign, he promised to address the weak economy, ethnic conflict, and terrorism.

A century of colonial rule and decades of military rule left a legacy of corruption and ineffective governance that democratic Nigeria has struggled to overcome. Still, some progress has been made toward a freer and fairer society. For example, elections in the 2010s and 2020s were observed by international experts and resulted in transfers of power without widespread violence. Nigeria has also improved its relationships with other democratic countries, benefiting from more international trade and aid.

CHAPTER **FIVE**

PEOPLE AND CULTURE

Nigeria is a land of more than 250 ethnic groups.[1] Throughout history, these groups have occupied specific geographic regions. Many still consider these regions to be their homelands.

The Hausa-Fulani, Nigeria's largest ethnic group, live in the northern part of the country. The Igbo people live in southeastern Nigeria. People of the Yoruba ethnic group make up most of the population in Lagos in the southwest. The Ijaw people live in the resource-rich Niger delta.

Today, migration around the country has softened some of those borders. However, specific languages and cultures still have strong influences in many

The population of Lagos, Nigeria's largest city, increased from 14.8 million to 16.5 million between 2020 and 2023.

In Kishi, Oyo, in eastern Nigeria, Fulani men are herders, while the women make and sell dairy products.

parts of the country. Additionally, the dominant ethnic group in an area often still controls local governments and the distribution of land in its territory.

NIGERIA'S NORTHERN PEOPLES

In the northern states, the Hausa and Fulani peoples predominate. They are sometimes referred to collectively as the Hausa-Fulani. The largest ethnic group in Nigeria, they make up about 36 percent of the population.[2] Hausa is the most common Indigenous language in this area. It is an Afro-Asiatic language spoken by more than 20 million people in western Africa.[3] Before colonial times, the Hausa traded with Arabic nations in the Middle East and North Africa. As a result, their language is written with modified Arabic characters.

The Fulani conquered the Hausa during the jihad in the early 1800s. Since that time, people from these two groups have lived together and intermarried. Most live in northern towns surrounded by farmland. The people rely primarily on agriculture to make a living, but many also practice a trade or art such as leather tanning or pottery making. Some Fulani have resisted intermarriage. They are mostly herders living in rural areas and are more likely to speak Fulani than Hausa.

The great majority of the Hausa-Fulani population is Muslim. The laws in several northern states are based on Islamic sharia law. Sharia law is derived from the teachings of Islam. It is a code of public and private duties that are believed to have been dictated by divine will. Under this law, men may have up to four wives. Women have limited access to education and public life.

Dress is colorful but modest, and most Muslim women keep their hair covered. The Muslim holidays of Ramadan, Eid al-Adha, Eid al-Fitr, and the Prophet Muhammad's birthday are important celebrations in this region.

A DIVERSE REGION

The greatest ethnic diversity is found in the central region of the country, including the plateau regions and the areas around the confluence of the Benue and Niger Rivers. The soils here are the least fertile in Nigeria. Still, most people rely on farming for their livelihood. The largest ethnic groups are the Tiv, who account for 2.4 percent of the population, and the Nupe.[4] Both groups speak languages that belong to the Benue-Congo family.

In a typical Tiv settlement, a man lives with his wife and children in a collection of small huts. Brothers live near each other and their father. While many have adopted Christianity and a lesser number follow Islam, the practice of their traditional religion is still common. The Tiv religion includes a belief in a supreme god as well as divine forces that influence people and the world around them. An elaborate system of ceremonies seeks to bring these forces into harmony and show obedience to the supreme god. Among the Tiv, elements of more than one religion are often mixed.

The Nupe live in villages and towns governed by a chief. While many are farmers, some are fishers. Many Nupe also practice skilled trades such as metalworking and weaving. Nupe artisans are respected for their glass beads, weaving, and leatherwork. Most Nupe are Muslims.

Tiv families traditionally live in round homes arranged in compounds. The Tiv are subsistence farmers who grow sorghum, yams, and millet.

However, the influence of their traditional religion, which includes belief in a sky god and spirits of ancestors and objects in nature, is still strong.

The Yoruba people are the dominant group of southwestern Nigeria, including Lagos. They make up 15.5 percent of Nigeria's population.[5] Most live in or near cities but own rural farmland. Groups of Yoruba are led by a chief called an oba, often in conjunction with a council. Traditionally they believed their people came from the city of Ile-Ife and were descendants of the divine king Oduduwa. Influences from precolonial times are strong among the Yoruba. The *ooni* of Ife, the spiritual leader, and the *alaafin* of Oyo, the political leader, still wield significant influence.

Oyo chiefs gathered to pay their respects to the traditional ruler of the kingdom of Ikere during a festival in the Ekiti State of Nigeria in 2024.

The Yoruba's traditional religion included the worship of hundreds of gods. Today, many Yoruba are Christians or Muslims but retain some traditional religious practices. The Yoruba language also belongs to the Benue-Congo family.

In rainforest regions of the southeast, the Igbo are the most numerous ethnic group, making up 15.2 percent of Nigeria's population.[6] Most live in villages governed by councils. Family groups own and farm land communally. The Igbo have a high English literacy rate, and many have taken government jobs or become entrepreneurs. Their language is part of the Benue-Congo family. Women are a strong influence in their local economy and politics. Most Igbo are Christians but retain elements of their traditional religion in which the central deity is Chineke.

AN EMERGING NATIONAL IDENTITY

The modern nation of Nigeria was created during colonial rule for the convenience of British administration. Its borders were determined largely by business and military interests. Its peoples do not share a collective history or culture that predates colonization. Even the name of the country was invented by colonizers. However, since independence in 1960, a national identity has slowly emerged, though significant ethnic and religious divisions remain.

One factor that is promoting a unified identity is the migration of Nigeria's people to urban areas. In 2024, a little more than half of Nigerians lived in urban areas. Beginning in the late 1900s, state capitals in particular grew rapidly. In these urban areas, people of different ethnicities are more likely to live side by side than in rural areas.

The official language, English, is also a legacy of colonization. Nevertheless, in a country with hundreds of Indigenous languages, it serves as a unifying way to communicate. About half of Nigeria's population speaks some English. That figure is likely to grow as English is increasingly the only language used on public signage and in government offices, broadcasts, websites, and schools.

Nigerians are also sharing more common pastimes and celebrations. Football, which is called soccer in the United States, is popular around the country. The men's national team is the Super Eagles, and the women's team is the Super Falcons. In 1996, the Super Eagles stunned the world by winning gold at the Atlanta Olympics. The team overcame ethnic tensions and a lack of support from the Abacha government to achieve what seemed impossible, becoming a symbol of hope for a better Nigeria. Today, support for the national teams crosses ethnic and religious lines.

National holidays celebrated across the country include Independence Day on October 1 and Labour Day, also known as Workers' Day, on May 1. Nigerians celebrate Independence Day with parades and fireworks. On Worker's Day, most schools and businesses are closed, and Nigerians often gather with family or friends to enjoy a day off. Some spend the day advocating for better wages or conditions for workers.

THE NIGERIAN NATIONAL WOMEN'S FOOTBALL TEAM

The Super Falcons are one of Africa's most successful football teams. Since the Women's African Cup of Nations began in 1991, they have won 11 of the 14 tournaments.[7] The team has also qualified for the Olympics in 2000, 2004, 2008, and 2024. In 2004, the team made it to the Olympic quarterfinals. The Super Falcons are also the only African team to qualify for every Women's World Cup since it began in 1991.

NIGERIAN ARTS

The arts are another way in which Nigerians express their identity. Dancing and drumming are important in most of Nigeria's Indigenous cultures.

Nigerian football fans turned out in droves to watch the men's national team take on Argentina during the 2018 World Cup in Saint Petersburg, Russia.

At the Osun-Osogbo Festival in Osogbo, Yoruba drummers and dancers perform to honor the goddess of fertility.

Traditional forms are still widely practiced. They are important features of celebrations and rituals, a form of storytelling, a way to build social bonds, and an expression of cultural pride. They have also given rise to new forms that transcend ethnic boundaries. Many of the dances made popular by Nigeria's Afrobeat and hip-hop musicians show influences of traditional dances. For example, the modern dance known as Zanku became a craze across Nigeria beginning in 2018. It reflects the energetic legwork of the Bata dance of the Yoruba.

Nigerians often mix elements of their heritage with modern techniques and aesthetics in the visual arts as well. For example, as sculptors and painters, both Ben Enwonwu and Yusuf Grillo

THE BENIN BRONZES

When British forces conquered the Kingdom of Benin in 1897, they looted an estimated 5,000 works of art that dated mostly from the 1200s to 1500s. Most famous are the plaques, sculptures, and ceremonial objects cast in bronze. Many ended up in museums and galleries around the world. One of those, London's Horniman Museum, is returning the 72 pieces in its collection.[8] Starting in 2026, the new Edo Museum of West African Art in Benin City will display the bronzes.

drew international recognition for their innovative work. They used European techniques to explore traditional subjects and motifs that reflected their heritage. Additionally, artisans across the country still produce leatherworks, weavings, jewelry, carvings, and metalworks, continuing the legacies of their ancestors.

Many pieces of that legacy were stolen by British soldiers during the colonial era. Since the 1930s, government and cultural institutions have worked to bring these stolen works back to Nigerian soil. Their efforts have secured the return of more than a thousand looted items from museums around the world.

TELLING NIGERIA'S STORIES

Several Nigerian literary figures have earned international acclaim. Among the best known is Wole Soyinka. As a young man in the late 1960s, he was an activist who opposed Nigeria's military government and its actions during Nigeria's civil war. For speaking out against the government, Soyinka was imprisoned and kept in near isolation for almost two years. Two decades later, in

1986, his plays, novels, and memoir called *The Man Died* were recognized with the Nobel Prize in literature. He was the first Black African to win the prize.

Poet and novelist Chinua Achebe is another Nigerian literary giant. His first novel, *Things Fall Apart,* was published in 1958, challenging European narratives about colonization. It also combined literary and oral storytelling conventions in an innovative way. In 1990, Achebe was paralyzed in a car accident, but he continued to write until his death in 2013.

Nigeria is home to the world's second-largest film industry. Dubbed "Nollywood" in a 2002 *New York Times* article, the nation's film industry is second only to the Bollywood film industry in India for total number of films made per year. Its films are produced in English and in several of the Indigenous languages of Nigeria. The advent of video streaming and widespread access to cell phones has spread the influence of Nollywood across the world. Nollywood films often center on escaping poverty and the impact of corruption or betrayal, themes that resonate with many Nigerians.

Nollywood produces about 2,500 films each year that together generate about $600 million in revenue.[9]

FLAVORS OF NIGERIA

Nigerians are adept at making simple ingredients, such as rice, beans, corn, and cassava, into flavorful, complex dishes. Soups, stews, and salads flavored with herbs, peppers, and onions are everyday fare. Jollof rice, a spicy dish that combines rice with tomatoes and peppers, is popular

GENEVIEVE NNAJI

Born in 1979 in southeastern Nigeria, Genevieve Nnaji is one of Nollywood's most prominent actors. She began her career as a child on a popular soap opera and appeared in her first film at 19. At the first African Movie Academy Awards in 2005, she won best actress for her role in *Darkest Night*. In 2018, she directed and starred in the Netflix film *Lionheart*. Her popularity is credited with helping to spread Nollywood's influence outside of Nigeria.

across Nigeria. Nigerian meals often include what Nigerians call a swallow food, a soft, doughy food that can be torn easily. Diners use the torn pieces to scoop up their stews or sauces.

Foods from various ethnic groups are crossing cultural lines to find wider popularity. For example, *suya* is a spicy meat, usually beef or ram, that is skewered and barbecued. It is often garnished with cabbage, onion, cucumber, and tomato. Suya originated in northern states where Hausa-Fulani herders raise sheep and cows. *Boli* or *bole*, a savory dish made from roasted plantains, came from the southwest, where the Yoruba are the predominant ethnic group. It may be served with fish, peanuts, yams, corn, coconut, or avocado. Suya and boli are now popular all over Nigeria.

The cultural divisions between Nigeria's various ethnic groups have a long history. However, the nation increasingly shares a common sense of place. In time, seemingly small gestures such as gathering to watch the Super Eagles take on Benin's national team may promote a nationwide sense of pride in being Nigerian.

CHAPTER **SIX**

POLITICS

Nigeria has been a presidential republic since its present constitution was adopted in 1999. That means national leaders are elected by Nigeria's citizens. All Nigerians 18 and older may vote.

As in the United States, the Nigerian government has three branches: executive, legislative, and judicial. All branches of Nigeria's federal government are based in Abuja, which is part of the Federal Capital Territory. Abuja became Nigeria's capital city on December 12, 1991.

BRANCHES OF GOVERNMENT

The executive branch is led by the president, who is also the head of state and commander in chief of Nigeria's military and security forces. Presidents are elected to four-year terms and limited to serving

Members of Nigeria's House of Representatives and Senate meet to discuss policy at the National Assembly Complex in Abuja.

Voters lined up to cast their ballots during Nigeria's presidential election in February 2023.

two terms. Elections may have more than two candidates. The winner must have the most votes across the nation and at least 25 percent of the votes cast in 24 of Nigeria's 36 states. This provision is designed to prevent the election of a president who is well-liked by one segment of the population but very unpopular with other groups.

In addition to the president, the executive branch also includes a vice president and the president's cabinet. The vice president is elected along with the president. The cabinet, called the Federal Executive Council, is chosen by the president. It must include at least one person from each of the 36 states.

NIGERIA'S NATIONAL ANTHEM

Independent Nigeria's first national anthem was "Nigeria, We Hail Thee." An English woman, Lillian Jean Williams, penned its lyrics. In 1978, the military government in power adopted a new anthem, "Arise, O Compatriots." Its words came from the top five entries of a national contest. However, in 2024 the National Assembly voted to change the anthem back to "Nigeria, We Hail Thee," citing a preference for the lyrics of the original anthem, which promote unity. Critics of the change said they want an anthem written by Nigerians.

The legislative branch is called the National Assembly and is bicameral. That means it is composed of two houses, or groups. One house, the Senate, consists of 109 members. Three senators are elected from each of the 36 states. One is elected in the Federal Capital Territory. Senators are elected by a simple majority and serve four-year terms.

The other group that makes up the National Assembly is the House of Representatives. It has 360 members, each elected from a single geographic area that is determined by population. Representatives also serve four-year terms. Women have historically been underrepresented in the National Assembly. In 2024, only 3.9 percent of the members of the National Assembly were women.[1]

In the judicial branch, the highest court is the Supreme Court. The number of justices on the court can vary but may not exceed 21, including a chief justice. A commission of federal and state officials nominates the justices. After their nomination, they must be confirmed by the Senate. Supreme Court justices may serve until the age of 70. In 2024, the chief justice was a woman, the Honorable Kudirat Motonmori Olatokunbo Kekere-Ekun. Nigeria also has a Federal Court of Appeals, and each state has a High Court.

The legal system uses a mix of customary law, sharia law, and statute law. Customary law is influenced by the historical legal practices of Nigeria's many ethnic groups. Generally it is administered in civil matters by local leaders. Some form of sharia law has been implemented in 12 of Nigeria's northern states.[2] The law is supposed to be applied only to Muslim residents of those states, with a parallel legal code for non-Muslims. However, non-Muslims argue sharia laws have a significant impact on their daily lives. For example, in some areas, women must ride on segregated buses and can't play sports. Statute law reflects Western legal ideals and is the strongest influence in state High Courts and federal courts.

The three branches of government have their seats in Nigeria's capital, Abuja. Lagos was the capital prior to 1991, but Nigeria's government moved its capital, largely to limit the political influence of any single ethnic group. The site of the planned city was chosen to allow for expansion. The area around the city was designated as the Federal Capital Territory and made independent of any state. Besides being home to government offices, it boasts multiple national attractions such as an arboretum, stadium, and zoo.

ALOMA MARIAM MUKHTAR

Born in 1944 in Lagos, Aloma Mariam Mukhtar attended law school in the United Kingdom. After graduating in 1966, she returned to Nigeria and went to work for a state Ministry of Justice. By 2005, she had worked her way up to Supreme Court justice. Seven years later, she became the first woman to lead the court as the chief justice. One hallmark of her service was fighting corruption in the judiciary system.

POLITICAL PARTIES

Nigeria has multiple political parties, but in 2024, the People's Democratic Party (PDP) and the All Progressives Congress (APC) were the most powerful. The PDP was formed in 1998 by groups that opposed the rule of dictator Sani Abacha. After Abacha's death in 1999, the PDP candidate won the first presidential election. That election marked the return of Nigeria to a democratic government. For the next 15 years, the PDP dominated Nigerian politics. The party's goals include decreasing economic regulations and promoting human rights, health care, and education.

The APC formed in 2013 when several groups that opposed the PDP merged. Their priorities have been curbing corruption, accelerating economic development, and increasing security in an era of domestic terrorism. The APC candidate won the 2015 presidential election, and the party held the presidency into the 2020s. The APC also won the most seats in both houses of the National Assembly between 2015 and 2023. After the 2023 election, it held 59 of the 109 Senate seats and 178 of the 258 seats in the House of Representatives. By comparison, the PDP occupied 36 seats in the Senate and 114 seats in the House.[3]

Since its return to democratic elections in 1999, Nigeria's elections process has been plagued by

NIGERIA'S STATE GOVERNORS

Each of Nigeria's 36 states is headed by a governor. Since many matters of law and policy are decided at the state level, governors wield significant power over the citizens of their states. They also influence which candidates are on the primary ballot for national elections. State governors are limited to two four-year terms, but many have gone on to become senators in the National Assembly or serve on the Federal Executive Council.

In the 2023 election, voter turnout in Nigeria was just 29 percent of eligible voters.[6]

charges of corruption and fraud leveled by parties, candidates, and international observers. Attacks on polling places sometimes prevented citizens from registering or voting. Violent conflicts between supporters of opposing parties led to deaths. One nonprofit, the Foundation for Partnership Initiatives in the Niger Delta, reported 161 fatalities due to election violence in 2023. That number was down from 240 in 2015.[4] As a result, Nigeria has adopted electoral reforms before and after every national election since 1999. Still, voter confidence and voter turnout remain low.

One reform, new biometric devices that verify a voter's identity, was employed in 2023 to help curb fraud. However, malfunctions with the devices on election day left voters skeptical about the benefits of the devices. A system designed to help polling places upload results quickly also faced glitches. In some areas, observers reported that polls did not open on time. There were also reports of voter intimidation and violence, though on a smaller scale than in previous elections.

A third party, the Labour Party (LP), gained popularity in advance of the 2023 election. A prominent politician, Peter Obi, left the PDP to become the presidential candidate for the LP. His campaign messages centered on economic opportunity, especially for young Nigerians. According to official results, Obi won almost as many votes as the PDP candidate. The PDP received 29 percent of the vote, and Obi took 25 percent. The winner, Bola Tinubu of the APC, won 37 percent of the vote. After the election, the LP also held eight Senate seats and 35 House seats.[5]

Posters promoting APC candidates Babajide Olusola Sanwo-Olu and Bola Ahmed Tinubu appeared throughout Lagos in 2022.

The result left supporters, especially young voters, hoping the LP would become a viable alternative to the two major parties.

SECURITY FORCES AND INTERNATIONAL RELATIONS

Nigeria's armed forces include an army, air force, and navy, including a coast guard. Nigeria also maintains a Security and Civil Defense Corps. Service is voluntary. The groups are primarily deployed to respond to terrorist groups within the country. The military and security forces also participate in fighting organized crime and large-scale theft at oil production facilities. The navy

In October 2020, protesters prayed in the streets of Lagos for an end to police brutality.

helps protect public and private vessels and offshore oil wells in the Gulf of Guinea. Combined, military and security personnel number about 215,000.[7]

The police force is managed at the federal level. Its force of more than 350,000 officers combats crime, handles disputes between ethnic groups and between herders and farmers, and provides security in public places.[8] Police are poorly paid and housed. As a result, morale is low and corruption is chronic. Many Nigerians fear harassment or brutality by the police.

Nigeria is influential in international relations, especially across Africa. It is one of 15 member nations of the Economic Community of West African States (ECOWAS).[9] This organization promotes free trade and economic development among its members and trading relationships and investment with international partners. To support its economic missions, it also has agencies that work to improve public health, security, and education. Its headquarters are in Abuja. Nigeria also plays an important role in the African Union (AU), a group of 54 African countries.[10] The AU seeks to promote peace, security, and social and economic development among its members.

The United Nations (UN) welcomed Nigeria just days after its independence in 1960. Since then, Nigeria has benefited from UN partnerships and expertise to assist its development. Nigeria has held one of the rotating memberships on the UN security council five different times and influences UN responses to conflict and humanitarian crises globally. About 150,000 Nigerian personnel have responded to at least 40 UN missions during its membership, ranking it fourth of all UN member states for its contribution of security forces.[11] Nigeria has also deployed troops to support ECOWAS and AU missions.

As a significant oil producer and a developing nation, Nigeria is part of the Organization of the Petroleum Exporting Countries (OPEC). OPEC coordinates policies between its 12 member nations with the goal of creating stable oil supplies and markets.[12] Its actions have a significant impact on the prices of petroleum products around the world, which in turn affect the world economy.

CHAPTER **SEVEN**

ECONOMICS

Nigeria has a mostly capitalist economy, meaning businesses are generally owned and operated by private individuals or companies. However, a few industries in Nigeria are controlled by the government. For example, the government owns rail lines and many radio and TV stations.

The oil industry, which has been the backbone of Nigeria's economy since the 1970s, is a hybrid industry. So is mining. The government owns all oil and mineral resources, and both private and government-owned companies participate in extracting and selling those resources.

In 2023, Nigeria's gross domestic product (GDP) was $363 billion. GDP is a measure of the total value of the goods and services produced in a region

Since 1956, crude oil production has been an important part of the Nigerian economy, accounting for about 6 percent of the country's GDP in 2024.

In December 2024, one US dollar was equal to about 1,577 Nigerian naira.

or country. It is a means of comparing the sizes of different economies. Usually, it is calculated for the period of a calendar year, and its change over time indicates whether an economy is growing, which is a sign of a healthy economy, or shrinking. Nigeria's GDP has shrunk from a high of $574 billion in 2014.[1]

Nigeria's currency is the naira. In April 2024, the annual inflation rate stood at 26 percent.[2] This means that products that cost 100 naira in April 2023 cost, on average, 126 naira in April 2024. A high inflation rate contributes to poverty because as prices go up, people can afford to buy fewer goods.

SERVICES AND AGRICULTURE

Services make up the largest part of Nigeria's economy. In 2023, they accounted for about 43 percent of Nigeria's GDP.[3]

Nigeria leads the world in cassava production, producing 69 million short tons (63 million metric tons) in 2021.

Health-care providers, schools, salons, and accounting and legal services are part of this sector. So are businesses such as theaters, restaurants, hotels, and tourist attractions. Nigeria has the potential to grow its tourism industry, but it is challenged by security concerns. In 2024, many foreign governments were advising their citizens not to travel in Nigeria due to unsafe conditions.

Agriculture accounted for 23 percent of Nigeria's GDP in 2023.[4] Yet the country does not produce enough food to feed its own people. Several factors contribute to the shortfall. In many areas, soils are poor or cannot be cultivated with machines. Where farmland is scarce, conflicts between farmers and herders often make land management difficult. Traditions resistant to selling family or tribal lands to outsiders sometimes cause land that could be cultivated to remain unused. In the far north, the desert is encroaching on what used to be agricultural land. Storage facilities and means of transporting goods are often poor, which makes it difficult to ship food between regions.

In central and northern states, the primary crops are legumes, such as cowpeas, and grains, such as maize, rice, sorghum, and millet. The south produces roots such as cassava and yams.

COCOA FARMING

Nigeria ranks fourth among cocoa-producing countries of the world. It accounts for 6.5 percent of the world's cocoa. The cocoa comes largely from cacao trees grown on plantations. Workers cut down the fruit of the tree by hand with machetes and then remove and dry the seeds to produce cocoa beans. The process requires many workers, who are often paid less than $1 per day and have no access to electricity or running water.[5]

Trees grown for agricultural purposes are also common in the south, including rubber, cacao, oil palm, and banana trees.

Herding is more common in the north. Animals raised for food include cows, sheep, pigs, goats, and chickens. Fishing is one of the fastest growing segments of Nigeria's economy, and the country is likely to become more dependent on fish as a source of protein as land for grazing animals becomes more scarce.

Though it accounts for less than a quarter of Nigeria's GDP, agriculture employs a much larger portion of the population. In fact, the United Nations estimates that 70 percent of the population engages in agriculture.[6] Most are subsistence farmers, though some work in commercial agriculture, such as at oil palm plantations. They often supplement their living by making household items or crafts, including soap, pottery, weavings, and leather goods. Bartering, or trading goods or services for essential items instead of paying money for them, is common as well.

OIL AND MINING

Oil was discovered in the Niger delta in 1956, and since the 1960s, Nigeria's economy has relied heavily on petroleum production. Petroleum products account for most of Nigeria's exports and are the largest source of revenue for the government. Some of that revenue comes from the activities of the government-owned Nigerian National Petroleum Company (NNPC) Limited. The company is involved in all phases of oil production and shipping. Newer efforts include producing cleaner energy sources such as ethanol, biodiesel, and solar energy.

The oil refinery in Kaduna, Nigeria, was being renovated in 2024 but was expected to produce 60,000 barrels of oil per day once fully operational.

The government also profits from collecting fees from international oil companies. These companies pay for the right to operate oil wells and refineries in Nigeria. Most oil is extracted in the Niger delta, but some wells are offshore in the Gulf of Guinea. Nigeria's oil production peaked in 2005 and 2006 at about 2.5 million barrels per day, but in April 2024 it was just more than one million barrels per day.[7]

Declines are due to many factors. Protests, strikes, and repairs have interrupted production. Oil wells and pipelines have been targeted for theft and terrorism. Poorly maintained equipment has caused spills. Due to concerns about these issues, several international companies sold their assets to smaller, local companies in the early 2020s. Whether homegrown companies could boost production and help grow the economy remained to be seen.

KAINJI DAM

The largest hydroelectric dam in Nigeria, the Kainji Dam, straddles the Niger River. Completed in 1968, it produces 760 megawatts of power. That's enough energy to supply about 626,000 homes at US consumption rates. The lake created by the dam submerged several towns and villages. The government moved about 50,000 people into newly built "resettlement villages."[8] Now the lake and dam provide water for irrigation, make the Niger River easier to navigate, and host a large national park.

Reliance on oil is a risk to Nigeria's economy. When oil prices are high, revenues are high, but when prices fall, it affects the whole economy. For example, when oil prices dropped in 2016, Nigeria entered a recession. The country's economy was hit hard again in 2020 when the COVID-19 pandemic caused a sharp drop in oil revenue as many people around the world stopped traveling and going to work.

Nigeria's other mined resources include natural gas, coal, tin, gold, and columbite. As with oil, the government owns all rights to mine these resources. Some mining operations are government owned. Privately owned companies pay the government for licenses to operate in Nigeria. In 2024, Nigeria announced it would grant new mining licenses to companies only if they also set up facilities to process the resources locally. The government hoped the policy would promote investments and create jobs.

INFRASTRUCTURE

Infrastructure includes the facilities and systems that provide power, transportation, and communication to a nation. Nigeria's infrastructure is growing, but it is still inadequate in many ways, making it incapable of providing a comfortable standard of living to all.

Nigeria has 37,000 miles (60,000 km) of paved roadways and 2,400 miles (3,800 km) of rail lines.[12]

Nigeria relies largely on oil and coal for power. These fuels are burned at power plants to produce electricity that is carried by power lines to homes and businesses. Disruptions to production occur at all points throughout the system, resulting in frequent power outages. In addition, about three-quarters of the rural population does not have any source of electricity.[9]

About one-fifth of Nigeria's power supply comes from hydroelectric plants at dams along the nation's rivers.[10] Abundant sunshine offers the potential for significant solar power generation. However, the technology and equipment needed to install solar power are scarce.

The nation's transportation infrastructure is insufficient for a country with an area and population as large as Nigeria's. By comparison, France is 40 percent smaller in area and has a population of less than a third of Nigeria's, but it maintains about 18 times as many miles of paved roads and seven times as many miles of rail lines.[11] Many Nigerian road and rail systems need significant repairs and upgrades. The inability to efficiently ship goods poses a major economic challenge.

Roads in Lagos are often clogged with traffic. The Lagos Metropolitan Area Transport Authority established rapid transit busing, which is used by 200,000 people each day.

In Lagos, residents had traditionally relied on motorbikes or kekes to move around. In 2022, the city banned motorbikes in much of the city, citing safety concerns. Yet the government has been slow to improve public transportation systems. Lines for public buses are often long. The first commuter train service didn't open until 2023. Many parts of the city are not served by any public transit. In Abuja, a commuter train opened in 2018. It was closed at the start of the COVID-19 pandemic in 2020 and did not reopen until 2024.

Abuja and most state capitals have airline services, but they are sometimes unreliable. Historically, airlines in Nigeria had poor safety records. However, safety standards are improving.

Several cities on the Gulf of Guinea are key ports for imports and exports that travel by sea. These cities include Lagos, Bonny, and Burutu.

TV and radio stations in Nigeria are mostly operated by the state governments. However, some privately owned stations exist. Very few Nigerians had phone or internet service prior to the spread of cellular phones in the 2000s and 2010s. Cell phones have also given most Nigerians access to TV and radio. Nigeria's 1999 constitution is supposed to grant freedom of expression and of the press. In practice, however, government-owned broadcasters often suppress critics. Federal and state governments have sometimes blocked certain websites and social media platforms to quell protests and criticism as well.

ECONOMIC CHALLENGES

Nigeria has a high birth rate. On average, women have about 4.5 children each. Life expectancy is low at 62 years. This has led to an increasingly young population. In 2024, about 40 percent of the population was 14 years old or younger. This means the workforce is rather small compared with the population, which can stress government resources and contribute to poverty.[13]

In 2023, the median age of Nigeria's population was just 19.2 years.[16]

As measured by government surveys, unemployment was 5 percent at the end of 2023.[14] This is a fairly low unemployment rate, but it doesn't tell the whole story. Only 15 percent of workers were earning wages from an employer.[15] The rest of the workforce worked for themselves or traded labor for goods. Additionally, subsistence farmers, herders, hunters, and fishers are not counted as part of the workforce, so they aren't included in unemployment statistics. Many of these workers live in poverty.

THE REMITTANCE ECONOMY

Nigerians who leave the country to find better jobs abroad often send money back to relatives still living in Nigeria. These payments are called remittances. In 2023, the value of remittances was about $20 billion. This amount exceeds the value of foreign investment and aid from foreign governments combined. It is an important segment of the economy, equivalent to more than 5 percent of Nigeria's GDP.[18]

Unemployment is also a much bigger problem for some groups than others. People between 15 and 24 years old and women are more likely to be unemployed than older workers and men. College-educated workers also struggle to find jobs in an economy that doesn't support enough highly skilled positions.

The poverty rate is perhaps a better indication of the economic hardships facing average Nigerians. About 56 percent of people live in poverty.[17] The number has grown as inflation makes necessities less affordable. These economic struggles lead to social problems. Families in poverty often cannot afford the fees or transportation to send their children to school. Without educational and economic opportunities, young Nigerians are more easily recruited to take part in criminal activities or violent conflict between religious or ethnic groups.

CHAPTER **EIGHT**

NIGERIA TODAY

Daily life in Nigeria varies significantly depending on a person's wealth, their gender, and where they live. According to the World Bank, the income of the top 1 percent of wealthiest Nigerians is 37 times that of the bottom half of the population.[1] The wealthy can access luxury goods such as expensive cars and jewelry. They also live in extravagant homes and can afford education and health care.

For those who live in poverty, just obtaining adequate food and a place to live is a challenge. In rural areas, those living in poverty are often subsistence farmers who struggle against drought and conflict to raise enough food to feed themselves. In urban

Young people in Nigeria are standing up for their beliefs. In 2020, many protested the police's Special Anti-Robbery Squad (SARS), which people accused of armed robbery, kidnappings, and killings.

areas, impoverished people often live in slums, which are crowded areas of a city with poor living conditions. They may be housed in small apartment buildings that are often damaged or incomplete or shacks made from scavenged materials such as wood, plastic, and cardboard. Nigeria's slums continue to grow as rural people move to the city in search of jobs.

Paying jobs are scarce, and people in slums often rely on bartering, begging, or theft to survive. In both rural areas and slums, people in poverty often lack basic sanitation. This means they don't have clean water sources, working toilets and sewers, and effective trash management. They also don't have reliable sources of electricity or health care. Because people live in close quarters with poor sanitation, slums have high rates of infectious disease. Mental health and substance use disorders are also common.

FAMILY TIME

Families are the most important cultural institution in Nigeria. Weddings are celebrated with large family gatherings, often including hundreds of guests. Traditions vary by ethnic group, but food, music, and dancing are enjoyed by everyone. Often, everyone in the bride's family wears a matching color, and the groom's family wears a different color.

Families also gather for funerals. Traditions associated with deaths are influenced by specific cultural and religious beliefs, but they often include music, singing, and dancing to wish the deceased happiness in the afterlife. In some instances, funerals may be delayed for weeks to allow relatives living outside the country to return.

Nigerian weddings often include several days of celebration, depending on the traditions of the couple's ethnic groups.

With family or friends, Nigerians enjoy going to restaurants, dance clubs, and sporting events. Besides football, Nigerians enjoy basketball and *dambe*, a combat sport similar to boxing. Watching movies and TV are also common pastimes. Like Nigeria's culture as a whole, these activities reflect a mix of traditional cultures and Western influences. They are available to most of the population due to the spread of affordable cell phone service.

Nigerian pupils study math, the English language, a Nigerian language, social studies, science, agriculture, physical education, and either Christian or Islamic religious studies.

EDUCATION

Under the law, six years of primary school and three years of junior secondary school are supposed to be free and compulsory. However, in practice, many children don't attend school. In 2024 the United Nations Children's Fund (UNICEF) found that 39 percent of primary school–age children were not going to school. At the junior secondary school level, 8.1 million kids did not attend school.[2] In some instances, students have no transportation to get to school. They may also leave school to work, or their families may not be able to afford the fees for school uniforms or supplies. Young men are sometimes recruited by terrorist groups or organized crime.

The situation is even worse in northern, majority Muslim states, where 47 percent of children do not attend school. In many cases, Muslim beliefs about education and the role of women discourage public education, especially for girls. Almost 53 percent of girls don't attend school in these states.[3] Some of these children who are reported as not attending school do attend religious schools that teach Islamic beliefs, but they do not study literacy or math.

In some states, terrorists have targeted schools. On April 14, 2014, Boko Haram kidnapped 276 girls from a boarding school located in Chibok in the state of Borno in the far northeast. They also burned the school to the ground. At least 20 of the girls were forced to marry Boko Haram fighters. In the following decade, many escaped or were rescued, but at least 82 were still unaccounted for in 2024.[4]

Attacks have continued since 2014. In 2022 and 2023, terrorists attacked 19 schools in the

THE UNIVERSITY OF LAGOS

Founded in 1962, the University of Lagos has become a top-ranked university in all of Africa. It serves more than 48,000 students.[5] Its first female vice-chancellor, Folasade Tolulope Ogunsola, was appointed in 2022 and is committed to making education more accessible to women and the poor. She also hopes to install solar power to provide a reliable source of electricity for the university.

northeastern states of Borno, Yobe, and Adamawa, prompting the closure of 113 schools. Between about 2010 and 2023, nearly 500 classrooms were destroyed by terrorists and religious-based violence. About 800 schools remain closed due to safety concerns.[6] Even where schools are open, families may be afraid to send their children.

Nigeria is home to more than 400 colleges, but graduates often leave the country to find jobs.[7] In the early 2020s, a large number of educated, middle-class young people left Nigeria, mostly for jobs in Europe and North America. The trend is called *japa*, which means "to break away" or "to flee" in Yoruba. Other young people leave Nigeria to go to college. They believe the quality of higher education is better in foreign institutions and that an education abroad will lead to better employment opportunities. These students are also part of the japa trend.

HEALTH CARE

Health care is one industry that has been hit hard by the departure of skilled workers. Nigeria has just a fraction of the doctors, nurses, and other health-care professionals it needs. The shortfall is not likely to improve soon, as these workers continue to leave for jobs with better pay and conditions in other countries.

Nigeria also needs more hospitals, clinics, and medical equipment, such as magnetic resonance imaging (MRI) and X-ray machines, to care for its population. The government has launched several partnerships with private companies to build more facilities, but most projects are still years from completion. If they can afford to, people often travel to other countries to get medical care.

Nigeria's health care system is one of the worst in Africa. The nation lacks modern medical facilities.

Pregnant women are especially vulnerable under Nigeria's strained health-care system. In 2020, Nigeria had the world's third-highest maternal mortality rate, largely due to inadequate health care.[8]

Cost is another significant barrier to obtaining health care. In 2018, just 3 percent of the population had health insurance.[9] Four years later, the government passed a law that requires all Nigerians to obtain health insurance and established a fund to pay for coverage for those who can't afford it. The government hopes to fully implement the law by 2030. Many humanitarian organizations, such as Doctors Without Borders and the United States Agency for International Development, run programs in Nigeria to provide health care to the most vulnerable. But ethnic violence in many parts of the country sometimes makes it challenging for these organizations to provide consistent help.

WOMEN'S RIGHTS

Women in Nigeria are more likely than men to be unemployed and illiterate. In states with sharia law, women have fewer rights to own property. Even where laws regarding land ownership are equitable, cultural traditions often keep women from owning land. Girls and women who marry at a young age have fewer economic and educational opportunities. Nationwide, nearly one-third of women are married by age 18. About one in eight are married by age 15.[10]

Violence against women is common. A study published in 2023 found that 28 percent of women between the ages of 25 and 29 had experienced violence since age 15, and 15 percent had experienced violence in the previous year.[11] Gender-based violence is fed by cultural norms and lax enforcement of laws against it. In some states with sharia law, it is legal for a man to beat his wife.

LGBTQ+ RIGHTS

In 2024, the advocacy group Equaldex ranked the LGBTQ+ laws and policies of 196 of the world's countries. Nigeria came in at 190. Same-sex marriage and relationships are punishable by prison sentences of up to 14 years in most of the country.[12] In some states with sharia law, they may be punished with death. Gender transition is also banned. LGBTQ+ people have no legal protection from discrimination.

FORCES FOR CHANGE

Nigeria faces challenges to create a free, fair, and secure nation. However, many Nigerians are working for change. Activism, especially among young Nigerians, is bringing some progress. One of their tools is social media, which has created a platform for raising awareness of issues and organizing activities to support change.

One example is the #endSARS movement from late 2020, which formed during lockdowns caused by the COVID-19 pandemic. Young Nigerians took to social media to protest brutality by a police unit called the Special Anti-Robbery Squad, or SARS. The movement sparked peaceful protests in cities around Nigeria, but the protesters often faced violent backlash from police. In one incident in Lagos, soldiers and police officers beat and shot at protesters. The number of deaths and injuries remains disputed, but one inquiry found 48 casualties.[13]

Eyewitnesses posted their accounts and videos of the clash on social media. Support came from around the world, bolstered by similar protests in other countries. The public outcry forced the government to disband the SARS unit. Some protesters felt the action did not go far enough or hold guilty parties accountable. However, many protesters and observers saw it as progress toward ending police brutality.

Climate change is another crisis facing Nigeria. Like most developing countries, Nigeria has contributed very little to carbon emissions, but it is already feeling climate change's impacts. Desertification in the north is reducing land available for agriculture, which is leading to conflict between ethnic groups. And in 2022, Nigeria experienced a wetter than usual rainy season that caused flooding in 34 states.[14]

Young Nigerians are also leading the way in climate action within the country. One such person is Martha Agbani, who works in the Niger delta. Her mother protested environmental harm caused by

The floods of 2022 displaced more than two million people, including about 800,000 children.[15]

MINI **BIO**

ADENIKE TITILOPE OLADOSU

Born in 1994, Adenike Oladosu is a native of Ogbomosho, a city in southwestern Nigeria. She earned a degree in agricultural economics. Even before she graduated, she was observing the impacts of climate change in Nigeria. She decided to do something about it. In December 2019, she attended the 25th United Nations Climate Change Conference of Parties (COP 25), an annual event that promotes international cooperation to fight climate change. Since then, she has led many efforts to counter climate change.

Oladosu's organization, I Lead Climate Action Initiative, works largely in the Lake Chad region. The group seeks to preserve the lake and help local communities adapt to changing resources. It also empowers Nigerian women to make a living despite climate change and gender injustice. Calling herself an ecofeminist, Oladosu educates people about the connections between environmental and gender issues.

Oladosu was selected as a finalist for the 2024 Pritzker Emerging Environmental Genius Award, which is given annually to someone under the age of 40 who is leading change on pressing environmental issues.

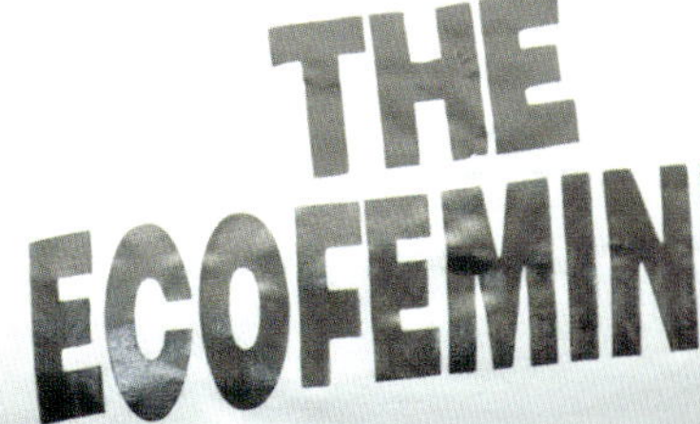

Shell Oil's drilling in the delta in the 1990s. Now Agbani has started a tree nursery. Her group plants mangroves where natural forests were destroyed by oil spills in the early 2000s. In addition to helping the environment, her work provides local women a means to make a living.

Like many young activists, Agbani sees a connection between gender and environmental justice. Nigerian women are more affected by environmental issues and climate change than men. This is partly due to their traditional roles in obtaining water and food for their households. Women are also less likely to be able to find a new way of making a living if their current one is threatened.

The problems facing Nigeria are complex, and many twenty-first century struggles have roots in the past. If the country is to have a brighter future, it will need its diverse people and government to work together to find solutions. Young Nigerians joining the fight for justice and opportunity choose action over cynicism and despair. They hope that choice will make a difference for Nigerians today and for generations to come.

MICROFINANCE

In developing countries, many small businesses and low-income individuals lack access to loans and banking services. Microfinance banks are helping to solve that problem. They provide services including loans and financial education. By 2021, microfinance had helped more than 40 million people in Nigeria with loans totaling more than $10 billion.[16] Loans help reduce poverty and create livelihoods for the poor, especially women.

ESSENTIAL **FACTS**

OFFICIAL NAME: FEDERAL REPUBLIC OF NIGERIA

GEOGRAPHY

Area: 356,669 square miles (923,768 sq km)

Highest Elevation: Chappal Waddi at 7,936 feet (2,419 m)

Lowest Elevation: Atlantic Ocean at 0 feet (0 m)

PEOPLE

Population: 236.7 million (2024 est.)

Most Populous City: Lagos (15.9 million)

Ethnic Groups: Hausa, Yoruba, Igbo, Fulani, others

Religions: Islam, Christianity, Indigenous belief systems

GOVERNMENT

Type of Government: Federal presidential republic

Capital: Abuja

Head of State and Government: President

Legislature: Bicameral, with a National Assembly consisting of a Senate and House of Representatives

ECONOMY

Currency: Naira

Major Industries: Services, petroleum production, mining, agriculture, manufacturing

Natural Resources: Petroleum, natural gas, coal, tin, columbite, farmland

NATIONAL SYMBOLS

National Anthem: “Nigeria, We Hail Thee”

National Animal: Eagle

National Motto: Unity and Faith, Peace and Progress

GLOSSARY

abolitionism
A social movement to free enslaved people and end the practice of slavery.

aesthetics
A set of principles or ideas about what is beautiful or meaningful in art.

annex
To take a part of land or territory, typically by force.

biodiversity
The many different plants and animals in an ecosystem.

black market
The illegal trade of goods that are banned or scarce.

columbite
A black mineral containing niobium, iron, and manganese that is often used in electronics.

coup
The overthrow of a sitting government, usually by military force.

divination
Seeking knowledge of the future through supernatural means.

encroach
To move into another being's or group's territory.

estuary
An area where river water meets sea water.

isthmus
A narrow strip of land with water on both sides.

jet lag
A feeling of exhaustion experienced after travel across multiple time zones.

recession
A period of economic decline.

separatist
A person or group determined to break away from a country and form their own nation.

subsistence farming
Growing only the amount of food needed for the farming family to survive.

tributary
A smaller river that flows into a larger one.

ADDITIONAL **RESOURCES**

SELECTED BIBLIOGRAPHY

Atwood, Roger. "The Nok of Nigeria: Unlocking the Secrets of West Africa's Earliest Known Civilization." *Archaeology Magazine*, 1 July 2011, archaeology.org. Accessed 18 Nov. 2024.

Biakolo, Kovie. "25 Years Ago, Nigeria's Super Eagles Won Olympic Gold—and Changed the World of African Soccer." *Time*, 2 Aug. 2021, time.com. Accessed 18 Nov. 2024.

"Nigerian Senate Approves Establishment of 10 New National Parks." *African Conservation Foundation*, 30 Mar. 2023, africanconservation.org. Accessed 18 Nov. 2024.

FURTHER READINGS

History of the World Map by Map. DK, 2023.

Kahumbu, Paula, and Claudia Geib. *Secrets of the Elephants*. National Geographic, 2023.

Natarajan, Radhika, and Chao Tayiana. *Hear Our Voices: A Powerful Retelling of the British Empire through 20 True Stories*. Wide Eyed Editions, 2023.

ONLINE RESOURCES

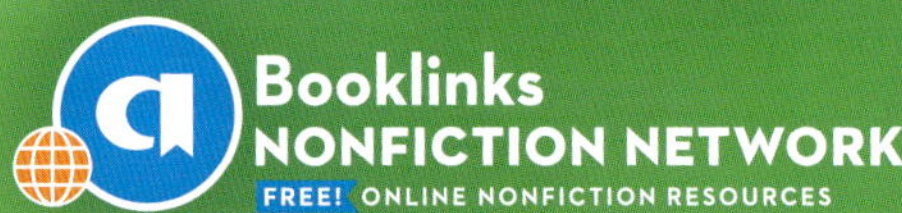

To learn more about Nigeria, please visit **abdobooklinks.com** or scan this QR code. These links are routinely monitored and updated to provide the most current information available.

MORE INFORMATION

For more information on this subject, contact or visit the following organizations:

Cross River Gorilla Programme

info@africanconservation.org
crossrivergorilla.org

The Cross River Gorilla Programme works with communities and organizations in Nigeria and Cameroon to protect the rainforest habitat of the endangered Cross River gorillas. It conducts field surveys, monitors wildlife, trains rangers and conservationists, and provides education for area schools.

I Lead Climate Action Initiative

2CW9+GH2 Metropolitan Area
Jabi, Abuja 900108 Federal Capital Territory
ileadclimateaction.org

The I Lead Climate Action Initiative was founded by Adenike Titilope Oladosu in October 2019. The organization leads grassroots efforts to address climate change in Africa, specifically in the Lake Chad region.

Nigerian Conservation Foundation

Km 19, Lekki-Epe Expressway
Lekki P.O. Box 74638
Victoria Island, Lagos, Nigeria
ncfnigeria.org

The Nigerian Conservation Foundation focuses on protecting the nation's ecosystems, species, and biodiversity, while ensuring that all future development is sustainable. Its goal is to build a Nigeria where people live in harmony with nature.

SOURCE **NOTES**

CHAPTER 1. A TOUR OF NIGERIA

1. Toyin O. Falola and Reuben Kendrick Udo. "Nigeria." *Britannica*, 8 Jan. 2025, britannica.com. Accessed 10 Jan. 2025.
2. "US Dollar to Nigerian Naira." *Western Union*, n.d., westernunion.com. Accessed 10 Jan. 2025.
3. "Lekki Market." *Tripadvisor*, n.d., tripadvisor.com. Accessed 10 Jan. 2025.
4. "Lekki Conservation Centre: Protecting Wildlife, Mangrove Forest from Urban Threat." *Daily Trust*, 12 Dec. 2020, dailytrust.com. Accessed 10 Jan. 2025.
5. Falola and Udo, "Nigeria."
6. "How Far Is Abuja from Lagos?" *Air Miles Calculator*, n.d., airmilescalculator.com. Accessed 10 Jan. 2025.
7. Chinedu Okafor. "The Top 10 Most Populated Cities in Africa in 2023." *Business Insider Africa*, 14 Mar. 2023, africa.businessinsider.com. Accessed 10 Jan. 2025.
8. Augustina Boateng. "Zuma Rock." *Atlas Obscura*, n.d., atlasobscura.com. Accessed 10 Jan. 2025.
9. "Super Eagles of Nigeria Stadium." *Super Eagles of Nigeria*, n.d., supereagles.sitesng.com. Accessed 10 Jan. 2025.
10. Omobolaji Durojaiye. "Kainji Lake National Park." *ConservationsNG*, 1 July 2024, conservationsng.com. Accessed 10 Jan. 2025.
11. "Kainji Lake." *Britannica*, n.d., britannica.com. Accessed 10 Jan. 2025.
12. Caitlin McLean. "Are Hippos Dangerous? What to Know about the Danger They Pose." *USA Today*, 21 Nov. 2022, usatoday.com. Accessed 10 Jan. 2025.
13. Durojaiye, "Kainji Lake National Park."

CHAPTER 2. GEOGRAPHY

1. "U.S. Census Bureau Current Population." *United States Census Bureau*, 10 Jan. 2025, census.gov. Accessed 10 Jan. 2025.
2. "Nigerian Geographical Information—Overview." *Embassy of Nigeria*, 2023, nigerianembassy.se. Accessed 10 Jan. 2025.
3. "Geography." *Nigeria High Commission in Ghana*, n.d., nigerianhcaccra.org. Accessed 10 Jan. 2025.
4. Augustina Boateng. "Zuma Rock." *Atlas Obscura*, n.d., atlasobscura.com. Accessed 10 Jan. 2025.
5. Toyin O. Falola and Reuben Kendrick Udo. "Nigeria." *Britannica*, 8 Jan. 2025, britannica.com. Accessed 10 Jan. 2025.
6. "Udi-Nsukka Plateau." *Britannica*, n.d., britannica.com. Accessed 10 Jan. 2025.
7. Falola and Udo, "Nigeria."
8. "Climate and Average Weather Year Round in Lagos." *Weather Spark*. n.d., weatherspark.com. Accessed 10 Jan. 2025.
9. "Lake Chad." *Britannica*, n.d., britannica.com. Accessed 10 Jan. 2025.
10. "West African Climate Activists at the Forefront of the Movement of Climate Justice." *Climate Reality Project*, 18 July 2023, climaterealityproject.org. Accessed 11 Jan. 2025.
11. "Maidurgi Climate." *Climate Data*, n.d., en.climate-data.org. Accessed 10 Jan. 2025.

CHAPTER 3. PLANTS AND ANIMALS

1. "Yankari Game Reserve." *Wildlife Conservation Society Nigeria*, 2021, nigeria.wcs.org. Accessed 10 Jan. 2025.
2. "Cross River National Park (Oban Division)." *Wildlife Conservation Society Nigeria*, 2021, nigeria.wcs.org. Accessed 10 Jan. 2025.
3. "Help Save Cross River Gorillas." *Cross River Gorilla Programme*, n.d., crossrivergorilla.org. Accessed 10 Jan. 2025.
4. "Cross River—Korup—Takamanda (CRIKOT) National Parks (Nigeria)." *UNESCO World Heritage Convention*, 2025, whc.unesco.org. Accessed 10 Jan. 2025.
5. Manuel Lopez-Bejar and Fernan Jori. "The Biology and Use of the African Brush-Tailed Porcupine as a Food Animal." *Biodiversity and Conservation*, Nov. 1998, researchgate.net. Accessed 10 Jan. 2025.
6. "Cane Rat." *Britannica*, n.d., britannica.com. Accessed 10 Jan. 2025.
7. Olajumoke A. Morenikeji. "Wild Fauna Conservation in Nigeria." *Environment and Natural Resources Research*, June 2015, researchgate.net. Accessed 10 Jan. 2025.
8. Morenikeji, "Wild Fauna Conservation in Nigeria."
9. Omobolaji Durojaiya. "Nigeria's Most Potent Snakes: An In-Depth Introduction." *ConservationsNG*, 13 Nov. 2023, conservationsng.com. Accessed 10 Jan. 2025.
10. "Nigeria." *AZ Animals*, 21 Feb. 2023, a-z-animals.com. Accessed 10 Jan. 2025.
11. "Guinean Forest of West Africa—Species." *Critical Ecosystem Partnership Fund*, 2025, cepf.net. Accessed 10 Jan. 2025.
12. John P. Rafferty. "9 of the World's Deadliest Snakes." *Britannica*, n.d., britannica.com. Accessed 10 Jan. 2025.
13. "Report on Malaria in Nigeria 2022." *World Health Organization*, 2022, afro.who.int. Accessed 10 Jan. 2025.
14. Paulinus Chukwamaucheya Aju. "Mangrove Forests in Nigeria: Why Their Restoration, Rehabilitation and Conservation Matters." *African Journal of Environment and Natural Science Research*, vol. 4, no. 1, 2021, 84-93, researchgate.net. Accessed 10 Jan. 2025.
15. "Okan (*Cylicodiscus Gabunensis*)." *Tropical Forest News*, n.d., tropicaltimber.info. Accessed 10 Jan. 2025.
16. "Nigerian Senate Approves Establishment of 10 New National Parks." *African Conservation Foundation*, 30 Mar. 2023, africanconservation.org. Accessed 10 Jan. 2025.
17. "Africa's Largest Ever Wildlife Awareness Program Launches in Nigeria." *WildAid*, 6 Jan. 2022, wildaid.org. Accessed 10 Jan. 2025.

CHAPTER 4. HISTORY

1. "The Transatlantic Slave Trade." *Harvard Divinity School*, n.d., rpl.hds.harvard.edu. Accessed 10 Jan. 2025.
2. "The Middle Passage." *National Park Service*, n.d., nps.gov. Accessed 10 Jan. 2025.

CHAPTER 5. PEOPLE AND CULTURE

1. Toyin O. Falola and Reuben Kendrick Udo. "Nigeria." *Britannica*, 8 Jan. 2025, britannica.com. Accessed 10 Jan. 2025.
2. "Nigeria." *CIA World Factbook*, 2 Jan. 2025, cia.gov. Accessed 10 Jan. 2025.
3. "About Nigeria." *African Studies Center: Boston University*, n.d., bu.edu. Accessed 10 Jan. 2025.
4. "Nigeria," *CIA World Factbook*.
5. "Nigeria," *CIA World Factbook*.
6. "Nigeria," *CIA World Factbook*.
7. Drew Vinestock. "Who Has Won the Most Women's AFCON Titles?" *Her Football Hub*, 30 Oct. 2023, herfootballhub.com. Accessed 10 Jan. 2025.
8. Emma Gregg. "The Story of Nigeria's Stolen Benin Bronzes, and the London Museum Returning Them." *National Geographic*, 17 Sept. 2022, nationalgeographic.com. Accessed 10 Jan. 2025.
9. Ivan Alberton. "Nollywood and Beyond." *Northwestern Libraries and Research Guides*, n.d., libguides.northwestern.edu. Accessed 10 Jan. 2025.

SOURCE NOTES CONTINUED

CHAPTER 6. POLITICS

1. "Nigeria." *CIA World Factbook*, 2 Jan. 2025, cia.gov. Accessed 10 Jan. 2025.
2. "Nigeria," *CIA World Factbook*.
3. "Nigeria," *CIA World Factbook*.
4. "Why Was Violence Lower in Nigeria's 2023 Election: Implications for Peacebuilding?" *Foundation for Partnership Initiatives in the Niger Delta*, 2023, fundforpeace.org. Accessed 10 Jan. 2025.
5. "Nigeria," *CIA World Factbook*.
6. "Nigeria," *CIA World Factbook*.
7. "Nigeria," *CIA World Factbook*.
8. "Fighting Organized Crime in Nigeria." *Interpol*, n.d., interpol.int. Accessed 10 Jan. 2025.
9. "About ECOWAS." *Economic Community of West African States*, n.d., ecowas.int. Accessed 10 Jan. 2025.
10. "The African Group." *African Union*, 2025, africanunion-un.org. Accessed 10 Jan. 2025.
11. Adeoye Akinola. "The Declining Role of Nigeria as Africa's Peacekeeper in the UN Security Council." *African Security*, vol. 17, no. 1-2, Jan.-June 2024, 59-86, tandfonline.com. Accessed 10 Jan. 2025.
12. "About Us." *Organization of the Petroleum Exporting Countries*, 2024, opec.org. Accessed 10 Jan. 2025.

CHAPTER 7. ECONOMICS

1. "GDP (current US$)—Nigeria." *World Bank Group*, 2025, data.worldbank.org. Accessed 10 Jan. 2025.
2. "Nigeria." *CIA World Factbook*, 2 Jan. 2025, cia.gov. Accessed 10 Jan. 2025.
3. "Nigeria," *CIA World Factbook*.
4. "Nigeria," *CIA World Factbook*.
5. "CAL and AFRILAW Document Widespread Forced Labor in the Nigerian Cocoa Sector." *Corporate Accountability Lab*, 17 Jan. 2024, corpaccountabilitylab.org. Accessed 10 Jan. 2025.
6. "FAO in Nigeria." *Food and Agriculture Organization of the United Nations*, 2025, fao.org. Accessed 10 Jan. 2025.
7. Doris Dokua Sasu. "Monthly Oil Production in Nigeria 2019–2024." *Statista*, 19 Aug. 2024, statista.com. Accessed 10 Jan. 2025.
8. "Kainji Hydroelectric Dam." *Institute of Civil Engineers*, 2025, ice.org. Accessed 10 Jan. 2025.
9. "Nigeria." *Federal Ministry for Economic Cooperation and Development*, 2 Feb. 2024, bmz.de. Accessed 11 Feb. 2025.
10. "Nigeria." *Britannica*, n.d., britannica.com. Accessed 11 Feb. 2025.
11. "Nigeria," *CIA World Factbook*.
12. "Nigeria," *CIA World Factbook*.
13. "Nigeria," *CIA World Factbook*.
14. Damilola Aina and Damilola Olufemi. "Nigeria's Unemployment Rate Rises to 5%—NBS." *Punch*, 19 Feb. 2024, punchng.com. Accessed 10 Jan. 2025.
15. Jonathan Lain and Utz Pape. "Why Do So Many Nigerian Workers Remain Poor? Labor Force Surveys May Have the Answer." *World Bank Blogs*, 6 Mar. 2024, blogs.worldbank.org. Accessed 10 Jan. 2025.
16. "Nigeria," *CIA World Factbook*.
17. "World Bank Reports Over 56% of Nigerians Living Below Poverty Line." *Africa Report*, 20 Oct. 2024, theafricareport.com. Accessed 11 Feb. 2025.
18. Dulue Mbachu. "Nigeria Relies on Diaspora Remittances for Economic Recovery." *African Business*, 3 Aug. 2024, african.business. Accessed 10 Jan. 2025.

CHAPTER 8. NIGERIA TODAY

1. Ode Uduu. "Nigeria's Wealth Inequality Score Is 35.1 and It's 11th in West Africa." *Dataphyte*, 25 Aug. 2022, dataphyte.com. Accessed 10 Jan. 2025.

2. "Nigeria: Education." *UNICEF*, n.d., unicef.org. Accessed 10 Jan. 2025.

3. "Nigeria: Education."

4. "Nigeria: Decade after Boko Haram Attack on Chibok, 82 Girls Still in Captivity." *Amnesty International*, 14 Apr. 2024, amnesty.org. Accessed 10 Jan. 2025.

5. "About University of Lagos." *University of Lagos*, n.d., unilag.edu.ng. Accessed 10 Jan. 2025.

6. "Nigeria: Education."

7. Toyin O. Falola and Reuben Kendrick Udo. "Nigeria." *Britannica*, 13 Jan. 2025, britannica.com. Accessed 10 Jan. 2025.

8. "Nigeria." *CIA World Factbook*, 2 Jan. 2025, cia.gov. Accessed 10 Jan. 2025.

9. Abiodun Awosusi. "Nigeria's Mandatory Health Insurance and the March Towards Universal Health Coverage." *Lancet*, Nov. 2022, thelancet.com. Accessed 10 Jan. 2025.

10. "Child Marriage in West and Central Africa at a Glance." *UNICEF*, Jan. 2018, unicef.org. Accessed 10 Jan. 2025.

11. Leon Usigbe. "Nigerian Women Say 'No' to Gender-Based Violence." *UN Africa Renewal*, n.d., un.org. Accessed 10 Jan. 2025.

12. "LGBT Equality Index." *Equaldex*, 2025, equaldex.com. Accessed 10 Jan. 2025.

13. "Nigerian Army 'Shot and Killed #EndSars Protesters': Report." *BBC*, 15 Nov. 2021, bbc.com. Accessed 10 Jan. 2025.

14. Rachel Stromsta. "Climate Change, Disasters, Insecurity, and Displacement: The Impact of Flooding on Youth Marginalization and Human Mobility in Nigeria." *International Organization for Migratio*n, 30 May 2024, environmentalmigration.iom.int. Accessed 10 Jan. 2025.

15. Stromsta, "Climate Change."

16. Olufisayo Adelekun. "Microfinance in Nigeria: The Key to Empowering Small Businesses in the Future." *LAPO Microfinance Bank*, 10 May 2023, lapo-nigeria.org. Accessed 10 Jan. 2025.

INDEX

ABOUT THE **AUTHOR**

RACHEL BITHELL

Rachel Bithell writes fiction and nonfiction for kids and their caregivers. Her debut middle grade novel, *Brave Bird at Wounded Knee: A Story of Protest on the Pine Ridge Indian Reservation*, won the Colorado Book Award for juvenile literature in 2024. Besides being a writer, she is a parent, teacher, and reader. Wole Soyinka's poems are among her favorites.